PERMISSION TO FLY

PERMISSION
TO FLY

A MEMOIR OF

Love, Crushing loss,

and Triumph

LAYNG MARTINE JR.

FieldPoint Press

For information, address FieldPoint Press, 305 Sutherland Avenue, Nashville, TN 37205

FieldPoint Press books may be purchased for educational, business, or sales-promotional use. For information, please email ATTN: Special Markets Department at bpuppy@ gmail.com.

First Edition

Designed by Gene Martine and Glen Edelstein
Library of Congress Cataloging-in-Publication Data has been applied for:

ISBN: 978-1-7320117-1-7

Author's Note

I have tried to recreate events, locales, conversations from my memories of them. In order to maintain their anonymity in some instances I have changed the names of individuals and places, I may have changed some identifying characteristics and details such as physical properties, occupations and places of residence.

For the loves of my life, Linda, Layngo, Tucker, and Mac

PERMISSION TO FLY

Introduction

Snuggled up in the middle seat of our family station wagon, I had my arm around the soft shoulders of my seventh grade girlfriend.

It was a cold Connecticut night in 1956 and my mom was driving us to the movies.

Suddenly, from the car radio I heard a new song.

A new voice.

A new sound...

I took my arm from around my girl and leaned forward.

"Mom," I said, "please turn it up, who is that?"

"I don't know," she said.

We listened until the song was over and the announcer said, "That was HEARTBREAK HOTEL by Elvis Presley, a young man from Tupelo, Mississippi."

A switch flipped in my heart and never went off.

In 2013 I was elected to the Nashville Songwriters Hall of Fame for writing songs recorded by Elvis Presley, The Pointer Sisters, Barry Manilow, Jerry Lee Lewis, Reba McEntire and others, all of whom I owe forever for giving me thrills and satisfaction far beyond my dreams and for making possible the free-spirited life I longed for. I had no musical training, and had to take an "incomplete" in my music theory class at Columbia University because I could not recognize or "hear" any of the triads and other musical figures played on piano by the professor.

I think the only reason I have been successful in music is that I've loved it with helpless passion and worked at it like a fiend.

As exciting and fulfilling as my songwriting career has been, this book is mostly about the challenge of finding an exciting and fulfilling life as a whole. I've been very lost at times and very wrong. Along with glorious highs I have hit wicked lowpoints, including bankruptcy and losing a house, the crippling of my wife in a car accident, a phone call telling me my brilliant music publisher had jumped off his 17th floor balcony, and a terrorist act that cost me a small fortune.

That said, I've been unbelievably lucky.

I was born in New York City in 1942, the oldest of five kids, a white boy in perfect health into a kind and happy family. My mom and dad paid for my college education, and for most of my life we lived in a wonderful house in a lovely neighborhood.

In other words, before lifting a finger myself, I had already caught about every wave you could catch.

Yet gradually, as early years slipped by, a baffling puzzle crept into my thoughts. Although I was growing up well off and in the "land of the free," no one around me appeared to actually be free.

At least, not the kind of "free" I wanted.

Among the people I knew, including my Dad, it seemed that most men's lives, certainly their days, were spoken for from the moment they got up until they got home at night. Where we lived, that meant driving seven miles to the railroad station to get on a train, riding the train forty minutes into New York City, and then either walking or taking a subway from Grand Central Station to the office.

For the most part, these men were highly educated products of places like Princeton and Dartmouth and Yale. The jobs they had, the exact nature of which I barely grasped in my young years, were clearly coveted, hard to get, and generators of good incomes. My dad always made it clear that he loved his job, but early on I began to question whether or not this life he and most other men I knew were living could possibly be for me.

My personal version of the life I did want unfolded before me the moment I heard the simple word "yes" from my mom the day she thought I was old enough to venture out on my own.

I was 8.

From that moment on, I wanted to be free like I felt on my bicycle. Free to go as far as my legs and my curiosity could take me.

Free to decide every day how I would spend that day.

But what on earth could provide that kind of freedom?

I had no idea.

Nor did I have any idea of the mistakes I would make and the prices I would pay as my curiosity and excitement led my search for such freedom.

I also had no idea how much help I would need along the way as I dreamed, and stumbled, and tried again.

I only knew I had to try my wings.

So, like a baby bird, as soon as I could peek over the edge of my comfortable nest and look around, my mom gave me permission to fly.

Chapter 1

To see my mom reading in her horn-rimmed glasses, or sitting behind the wheel of her station wagon, or at church in her Sunday best, you'd never have guessed she was virtually fearless and immune to convention.

But she was.

And her open-minded courage was my lasting gift.

She made me believe I could handle anything that happened, so she never rescued me.

She convinced me I could cope, figure it out, rescue myself.

So I tried everything.

At least, everything that interested me.

"Why not?" she said, "if it doesn't work, try something else."

With extreme respect for others' ways of thinking, Mom had no trouble relying on her own ideas and sensibilities whether or not they lined up with prevailing norms and she encouraged me to do the same.

Her unique turn of mind played out in ways large and small.

On weekend mornings Mom and Dad enjoyed the freedom of their own home and both usually went around the house wearing nothing at all. That went on for years. Sometimes a friend would walk in without knocking and see one of them cooking breakfast or vacuuming in the nude.

Kids in the neighborhood never quite got used to it.

One day a friend walking on the road below our house and far out of my sight called up through the trees, "Hey Layng, I'm coming up there, is your mother bare ass?"

Apparently, this comfortable style continued long after I got married and moved out. It made a lasting impression on people.

My sister Anne is ten years younger than me.

She's now 64 and last summer I ran into one of her high school friends at a party.

He smiled and walked over when he saw me.

"Hey, Layng," he said, "your parents put their clothes on yet?"

So far, I've done no cooking or vacuuming in the nude, but Mom and Dad's early example of free-form thinking has definitely made thinking for myself no problem. And, alongside their harmless offbeat behavior and original, very thoughtful child-rearing, in most ways our parents were traditional, ultra-responsible, with high hopes and expectations for their children, and as normal as you can be while raising five kids and surviving Mom's eventual nervous breakdown.

When I was born in 1942, I suppose we were middle class even though there was little money around.

I say middle class because both my parents were college educated, we lived in a nice neighborhood in the Bronx, and both parents had good jobs, good prospects.

Mom wrote for a movie magazine and Dad solicited advertising for a magazine called *Baby Talk*.

Then, a few months after I hollered my way into the world, Dad shipped off with the Navy to the South Pacific and World War II.

He was gone for years.

I heard about him, asked about him, saw pictures of him, and wished he would come home.

One morning when I was 3, I packed a pair of short pants, a shirt, and some underwear into Mom's big suitcase, skidded it down the stairs, across the kitchen floor, and out the back.

I had dragged her old leather bag fifty feet through the grass toward the road when she saw me and opened the screen door.

"Layng," she called, "where are you going?"

"I'm going to the war to find my dad," I said.

She burst into tears, ran, wrapped her arms around me and carried me inside.

I've always thought that had I been a few years older she'd have probably told me to go for it. That's because as I grew up she often said "Yes" to ideas and adventures that appalled most parents. So except for "I love you, Layng," of all the things Mom ever said, my favorite was when she said "Yes."

She was one who gave you more than enough rope to trip yourself, while hoping and trusting that you'd do just fine.

Mostly I did just fine and mostly when I didn't she never knew about it because the whole idea was to learn to handle things myself.

With Dad gone, Mom's father was the most visible man in my life.

He was an imposing person.

In 1909, when William Howard Taft was president and before beginning his banking career, Grandfather was the youngest member of the United States Congress.

He carried himself like somebody who is used to winning, one who expected to govern his world, and maybe yours, too.

He had a 1000-acre farm in the Adirondacks and even when I spent a summer week up there with him he always wore a suit, vest, and pocketwatch and on the quarter of every hour he needed to be near a radio to hear the stock market report.

I always thought the farm was worth a fortune. But when Grandfather died, my mom and her sisters couldn't even get an offer on it so they gave it to the Boy Scouts of America.

Grandfather had a chauffeur, named Randolph.

Randolph may have come with Grandfather's job as president of a small bank in New York City. I don't know.

In any case, Randolph and I became related, or so we decided.

He was the first person to take me to a Yankee game and, later, to a grown-up Western movie. The movie starred Randolph Scott and in it a bad guy was tied to two different horses which were then struck with whips and sent in different directions, pulling apart the bad guy.

Even though Randolph assured me that it was "just in the movies" and didn't really happen, I had nightmares for weeks about the guy being pulled apart. Randolph didn't take me to any more movies.

But he did everything else with me, including catch what I thought was a baseball pitch far too fast for any human being to handle.

Each time he caught one of my pitches, Randolph would squint as though in great pain and shake his catcher's glove and say something like "I may have to go to the hospital!"

Then he would shoot me a big smile.

Randolph's tight curly black hair was cut in a pompadour, making a neat "bump" right in the front.

For some reason I couldn't take my eyes off that bump.

When I was about 4 he said, "Do you want to touch Randy's pompadour?"

I did.

And I think I was probably 12 before he stopped asking me that.

It was one of our bonding elements.

I don't think he ever asked me if I wanted to touch his pompadour when I didn't say, "yes."

Years after my grandfather died, I saw Randolph on 57th Street in Manhattan holding open the door of a black Cadillac limo for a well-dressed woman.

Though I was 23 at the time Randolph picked me up off the sidewalk, flung me in the air and said, "My Layng!"

He put me down and we looked at each other.

In every way that mattered, I was still "his Layng" and I said so. If only with my eyes.

It was the last time I saw him.

I often wonder if Grandfather left Randolph a little money.

I hope so, though I don't know if subtle generosity outside the family was his strong suit.

But in 1940, when my parents married, Grandfather was the force to be reckoned with in our family and remained so in my parents' early years of marriage. He was a strict Catholic, with all that implies: church every Sunday and no birth control beyond the "rhythm method" — that is, attempting to skip sex on the most fertile days of the month.

Grandfather also had the money to give my parents $10,000 which they used to buy eight acres of land when Dad got home from the war, helping to give them a solid start in life. They promptly sold off two acres to raise cash and built us a new house on the highest point of the remaining six.

Thanks to my dad's independent nature, Mom gradually crept out from under the iron spell of her father's rigid Catholic ways and broke free. But not before its power had taken a great toll on her.

During the war years with Dad away, money was scarce and even though Mom's job at the movie magazine often required her to be in New York City to interview stars and see new movies, we moved out of the City about an hour to a house in a rural part of Stamford, Connecticut because rents were cheap.

My first hint that my grandfather's influence over Mom was waning was on a day he was coming out there to visit.

Upon climbing out of his black, chauffeured Oldsmobile he would always say, "My boy, have you been going to church on Sundays?"

To date, I had always said yes or no depending on the truth of the matter. But if my answer was "No," a form of hell would soon descend on Mom.

On this particular visit, before my grandfather arrived and since we had not been church-regulars lately, Mom said, "Layng, today if your grandfather asks if you've been going to church, say 'Yes'."

Given that my Mom was, and remains, the paragon of honesty and fair play, this request was my first clue that sometimes a lie is best for everybody and that even models of goodness tell them once in a while.

Mom was also my personal, living definition of human spirit and lust for life.

One Sunday morning in 1945, she and I came out of St. John's Cathedral in Stamford and walked across the street to a news store where Mom bought *The Sunday New York Times*.

Something on the front page grabbed her attention and she stepped to the side and started reading.

Suddenly the paper and both her arms shot up in the air, she shouted, "WOOOOOOOO!!!!!!! OHHHHHH, GOD!!!!!!!!!!!

"DADDY'S SHIP!" she hollered, "IT'S COMING IN!!! HE'S COMING HOME!!!!!"

Everyone near us stopped to look at the woman who had just publicly lost her mind.

Mom was smiling and crying when she took my hand and led me to the back of the news store, which was all toys.

She asked the salesman to show her an "express wagon."

Five minutes later I was sitting in a wooden wagon with the Sunday *Times* on my lap as Mom zoomed us down the sidewalk through the Sunday strollers and churchgoers, waving and crying, "He's Coming Home!!!"

I can't imagine how much of her meager monthly budget was blown on that wagon.

I don't remember the moment Dad walked through the door, but I remember how our life changed.

For one thing, Dad, and not Mom, mowed the grass. And sometimes my parents had parties that would go on long after I was in bed. After so long with the quiet of just Mom and me, I loved lying in the dark and hearing the laughter and conversation. The next morning there would be lots of glasses on the mantelpiece and on the coffee table, some with cigarette butts and an inch of light brown booze still in them…and a smell of stale wet ashes.

At age 4 or 5, that's what a good party looked and smelled like the next day.

I don't remember Mom saying we were short of money after Dad got home.

Some weekend mornings I would climb in bed between the two of them and they would both put their arms around me. I felt warm and safe snuggled there together, and I can remember thinking that they smelled like grownups.

I also remember being in the back seat of our car and watching the gas pump spinning gallon after gallon into our tank until it was full, something that hadn't happened much during the war.

Dad's new job was in New York working for Dell Comics. He took the train into the City every day. Once I went to his office and Mr. Dellacorte, the owner of Dell, took me into a room where we stood surrounded by three-foot piles of that month's comic books.

"You know what these are?" he said.

I looked around.

"Comics!" I said.

"Right," he said, "Dell Comics. Do you like Mickey Mouse and Donald Duck?"

"Yes, and Bugs Bunny and The Lone Ranger and..."

My eyes shot everywhere.

I couldn't read, but I knew all the characters. Long before TV, the colorful rectangles on each page of a comic book told a story you could follow whether you could read or not.

That day I held my arms out straight and Mr. Dellacorte stacked up almost more of these magical stories than I could carry.

I was extremely proud to tell other kids my Dad was associated with the likes of Mickey and Donald and Bugs.

One night, not long after Dad got home from the war, Mom and I went to the Stamford train station to pick him up. When he got into Mom's old blue Pontiac we drove 200 feet across the parking lot to Thompson Motors, the Pontiac dealer, where we gave them our old blue car and they pulled up a new maroon 1947 Pontiac convertible right in front of us.

Mom and Dad looked at each other and beamed.

"Doesn't this seem impossible?" Mom said to Dad.

"It does," he said.

I was in shock.

"This is our car?" I said.

"Yes," said my dad.

I climbed in the back and couldn't believe how huge the seat was and how good it smelled.

Leaving the big brightly lit garage Dad spotted Alfred Weld, a friend who lived near us in the country, and we drove him home. From then on, even as a teenager, any time I rode my bike past Alfred Weld's house I thought of the night we dropped him off in our new Pontiac.

We had the convertible for three years, long enough for all of us to get very tan on summer rides and to accidentally back over our female pointer named Gal who lay in my arms bleeding and drooling on my bare legs as we sped her to the vet where she was saved.

When my brother and sister were born we sold the convertible and bought a second-hand station wagon from our neighbors. The station wagon had real wood on the sides that sometimes mildewed and made the sides look old and rotten. When that happened my dad would park the car in the driveway and sand down the wood until he hit bright new layers and then brush on coats of varnish until the station wagon looked showroom-new.

Dad could do most anything around the house. One of the many differences between us.

When I was 8 and they were planning our new house, my dad, by himself, built a guest house: foundation, walls, electricity, heat, roof and windows.

The land on which they built these two houses was a few minutes' walk down the same country road where we'd been living.

When they bought the property they decided to have the house designed by a "Modern Architect." The "modern houses" designed by this school of architects often had flat roofs, lots of glass, and were mainly on one floor. They were a new thing after the war and several men were getting famous as "Modern Architects." Two of those people were Marcel Breuer and Edward Durrell Stone. Before they both got unreachably famous and expensive, either one could be hired affordably by a successful young family.

On separate occasions both Breuer and Stone took the train out from New York City to meet with my parents and see the land, the setting, and to exchange ideas.

Both made models of the houses they proposed.

For some reason, my dad got upset with Marcel Breuer and ended up choosing Stone.

The house Stone designed had exposed beams, floor-to-ceiling living room windows, radiant heat in the brick floors and a huge stone fireplace.

I thought it was unquestionably the coolest structure ever built.

Much of my devotion to that house was due to my watching nearly every stick, stone, and brick go into it, daily riding my bike to the building site seconds after debarking the school bus, and grilling every carpenter onsite as to the exact reason for each tool he used and on the origin of every plank.

One carpenter, Steve Hudson, was a young guy I thought especially cool.

Steve had something he said to me most every day.

It was, "Hey, I hear your mother calling!"

I didn't know that was Steve's way of telling me to get lost.

My Dad had a keg of beer set up 24/7 for the workers and one of my earliest associations with that house is the smell of beer mixed with sawdust.

Sometimes I'd draw a beer and drink a little, but I never craved it.

Long before we even broke ground on the house's foundation all of us would ride over to the property on weekends.

Sitting on the edge of the station wagon's tailgate for the short trip, my younger brother and I would swing our legs back and forth, nearly touching the road, daredevils to the core.

To my 8-year-old eyes, our new property was boundless. In summer, we couldn't see another house. The land had stone walls and fields, a creek, a million trees and gigantic boulders to explore.

Some Saturdays before the house went up Mom and Dad would lie in the grass. They'd both take off their shirts and sunbathe in their shorts, Dad bare-chested, Mom in her bra.

Relaxed as they were on some things, though, not so on everything.

One Thanksgiving I came home with a horrible report card.

"Mom, the teacher hates my guts."

"Work it out, Layng," she said, "you're stuck with each other."

Once, I threw a rock and accidentally broke the window of a neighbor's greenhouse.

I was a nervous wreck and told my parents.

"Did you tell Mr. King you broke his window?"

"No."

"Go knock on his door, tell him you broke his window and you'll pay to have it fixed…with your salve money."

My "salve money" was money I earned selling Cloverine Salve door-to-door in our neighborhood. I got the Cloverine Salve by sending away to an address on back of one of my comic books, comics that now filled large cardboard boxes in my room.

The deal with the Cloverine Salve was that you sent in your name and address and they sent you the salve, 12 cans, and after you sold all 12 you sent the company back a share of the money.

I sold a lot of salve and also a lot of Christmas and greeting cards, depending on the season, ordered the same way.

From selling the salve and the cards, I learned that if I just kept knocking on doors I would eventually sell out of whatever I was selling. Some nights as it got dark and I was about to quit for the day I'd pass a house and say, "Let me try just one more."

Often, that "one more try" led to one more sale after that.

That "try just one more" work pattern has come in handy for about everything I've ever done since.

CHAPTER 2

The year I was 8 I wanted a steady job so I'd always have ready cash and never have to ask my parents for the extra things I wanted. I hated to ask. And my constant requests to buy "essentials" like eclairs, Tootsie Rolls, popsicles, a different baseball bat, baseball cards, a bell or streamers for my bike, or film for my camera and money to develop the pictures, would have been such an endless a stream of "gimmies" that I probably wouldn't have broached the requests at all, thereby severely cramping my freedom and exploration.

It was much more pleasant to have my own money.

Because there were only two businesses in our immediate neighborhood and one was a gas station, the local restaurant seemed the best possibility. The guy who owned the restaurant was known to be an odd duck, but I figured there had to be some undesirable job around the dining room and kitchen suitable for a little worker-bee kid.

The next Saturday morning I rode my bike up the hills, through the village, past the two white wooden churches and the houses from the 1800s, past the volunteer firehouse with its large square-dance platform in back, and around the corner to the Country Kitchen, the popular restaurant in an old red barn where I put down my kickstand and went inside to find proprietor Ian McPatrick.

I pulled open the heavy red door, saw myself reflected in the door's small windows and was glad I'd put on a white shirt.

It was about 9:30 a.m. and inside the place looked empty.

A slim older man walked out of the kitchen carrying glasses.

"Hi," I said, "is Mr. McPatrick here?"

"Dining room," he said.

I looked around and through a doorway saw a big room with linen tablecloths and glasses on lots of tables.

I walked in and saw a slight, curly-headed man at a table surrounded by papers, furiously writing with a pencil.

I stepped closer and closer but he never looked up.

At his table, I stopped.

"Hi Mr. McPatrick, I'm Layng Martine."

He was startled and looked up.

"How the hell did you get in here?"

"I walked."

"Jesus," he said, "what do you want?"

"A job," I said, "I'm a very good worker, thought you might need someone to help you."

"Help me? Do what?"

"Jobs around here, whatever you need."

"What? You're too goddam young," he said. "Sit down, I'll bring you a Coca-Cola."

I pointed to the man setting out glasses.

"I can do whatever that man's doing…"

He looked at him, back at me.

"How old are you?" he said.

"Eight."

"Eight! I'd get arrested if I hired you."

I stood there a minute.

Then I smiled.

"Some people think I'm ten."

"Ten!" Now he smiled, "No! Get your ass out of here."

That day I rode my bike home, climbed up into my tree hut, lay down in the sun and closed my eyes to regroup.

"He's crazy," I thought.

I decided I'd offer to up my workload around the house and see if Mom and Dad would give me at least a semi-hefty boost in allowance in exchange for adding car-washing and weeding to my present assignment of mowing the field in front of our house.

That's also when I started sending away for the Cloverine Salve and assorted greeting cards advertised on the back of my comic books because I could sell those things door-to-door with no age requirement to stop me.

Then, a few years later, Mr. McPatrick saw the light.

"Oh, for Christ's sake," he said when I walked in the door.

"I'm 12 now," I said.

"Twelve! And what do you want to do?"

"Work. Make money."

"Oh, Jesus," he said looking right at me.

Then he turned around a few times looking up at the ceiling.

He tapped his fingers on the bar and stared at me sideways.

"You know," he said, "if you're a pain in the ass I'm going to send you home."

He hired me as a busboy, and I made a whole lot of money working for him.

Enough money to fill milk bottles with silver coins and take my friends on extravagant bike rides, during which we'd stop at country stores and village bakeries, trade baseball cards on the stores' loading docks and luxuriate on their front steps with popsicles, eclairs, and Napoleons.

At that stage, few of my friends worked and, because the bike rides were often long and strenuous, if I wanted a riding buddy I often had to bribe them with the promise of funding their treats along the way.

I didn't care. There was a lot more where that came from.

Apart from the gourmet bike rides, Mr. McPatrick's employ afforded me baseball gloves, a sleeping bag, Boy Scout canteen, combat boots and other elements critical to my budding lifestyle.

Sometimes a diner would motion me over and slip me a quarter or two, heavy, cold and solid in my hand.

"You're doing a great job, son," they might say, or something similar.

Such moments made me feel valuable and appreciated.

But every few weeks Mr. McPatrick would fire me. The reasons varied.

He had a bunch of birds in the restaurant. All in cages. We were supposed to feed them, but never let them out.

"Don't let the goddam thing out!" he'd holler anytime we'd open the cage to drop in a ball of bird suet. Nobody liked to drop suet when Mr. McPatrick was around because he always wigged out like that, even though there was no danger of an escaped bird.

Even so, we all got paranoid that we'd be the one to let one of the birds loose and there'd be hell to pay.

One Saturday night the restaurant was packed, waiters nearly colliding as they barreled through the in-and-out kitchen doors, the bartender mixing and pouring like crazy to keep up, and Mr. McPatrick unusually frantic and anxious to please.

Amid the chaos, a regular customer asked if he could hold one of the birds.

That wish normally generated a quick "No!" from Mr. McPatrick, but he was pretty boiled by then and opened the cage.

V-e-r-y slowly Mr. McPatrick eased the tiny grey bird out on his finger and, as its yellow-tipped tail twitched wildly, Mr. McPatrick handed him proudly to the big, round-faced customer.

The jowly fatman smiled, wobbled slightly, held the bird in one hand and tried to pet him with the other.

Suddenly the bird took off.

He flew like a shot into the dining room full of eaters. Mr. McPatrick raced in after it as the bird sailed into a delicate arrangement of antique glass vases, splattering them in tinkling pieces across the floor. Men ducked, women screamed. Mr. McPatrick turned around to me and hollered "Catch that son of a bitch!"

As the bird wreaked havoc darting terrified in straight lanes back and forth and up and down the room, a few people shot up from their tables when they saw an opening and ran for the exit. As luck would have it, one diner pulled on the door just as the bird needed it opened and the tiny finch fired silently off into the darkness.

The deed done, a sigh of relief fell over the dining room.

For all but Mr. McPatrick. He was apoplectic.

His curly hair was wild, his eyes in a fury, sweat poured off him like he'd just run a marathon.

I looked at him.

He looked at me.

"You're fired, for Christ's sake, get your ass out of here!" he bellowed in front of 40 shellshocked diners.

"I didn't let him out," I said.

"You didn't catch the son of a bitch, either!" he said and turned on a dime.

I took off my apron and put it on the bar and rode my bike home.

The next morning at a little after 11, the phone rang. It was Mr. McPatrick.

"It's 11:15, where the hell are you?"

"You fired me last night."

"That doesn't mean a damn thing, get your ass in here, we've got to serve lunch."

Our relationship continued on like this for quite a few years. One way or the other, I figured out what did and did not mean anything to Mr. McPatrick, so most of his bull and bluster slid pretty easily off my back because I knew that, way past it all, he liked me.

When I got older and needed quick money for gas or girls he was always a soft touch.

He lived above the restaurant, in the top part of the barn on the second floor.

I'd climb the wooden stairs to his apartment and knock on the door.

Mr. McPatrick would stick his head out, hair a mess.

"What the hell do you want?" he'd say.

"Can I wax the car?"

"How much?"

"Fifteen bucks."

"Jesus. All right. Let me get the money."

He always paid in advance.

I knocked myself out to make the car beautiful. It was a red Ford convertible and I loved it.

Then I went off to boarding school and wasn't home much.

In the meantime, Mr. McPatrick opened a fancy French restaurant called "The Arch" about 20 miles away in Armonk, New York.

The Arch was small, only about eight tables, and the prices were high. The highest. But for the money you got mood, you got food, you got candlelight and time, and you got service.

Rave reviews spread quickly.

Even though it was a 30-minute drive from our Connecticut hamlet, The Arch became the high-five, go-to place for adults when they were really putting on the dog.

If someone said, "We're going to The Arch Saturday night," that was Flash. That was Paris in the Woods. That was, "I'm rich and I love you."

My first weekend home from the Army I went there with my wife. It was our first time. I wore my uniform. Mr. McPatrick gave us the best seat in the house. We had wine, salads, lobster bisque, steak au poivre, crème carmel and Irish coffees.

When our waiter brought the bill we were shocked. It was for $17.00. Even then, that was peanuts.

For that token charge, Mr. McPatrick had basically treated us.

We had no idea the extent of his treat.

Of course, the next time we went we brought a lot of money.

It was a year or two later and I was no longer either a kid or a soldier.

We were grown-ups. Now in our mid-20s. We brought our friends Chuck and Marilyn and wore jackets and ties and dresses and had another equally lavish and scrumptious meal.

Even though Chuck and I had shown up with a wad of cash, the event cost much more than we expected.

I went and found Mr. McPatrick.

"Mr. McPatrick, may I write you a check? We thought we'd brought enough money but we were wrong."

He smiled.

"Is the check any good?"

"Yes, it's good."

"If it bounces you're gonna have to wax my goddam car," he said.

It was the last time I saw him.

A few years later I heard he'd sold The Arch and moved to Alicante, Spain to open a new restaurant and live out his life in the sunshine.

Not long afterwards, his obituary appeared in our local paper.

I wish I had seen him. I wish I'd gone and told him how often I thought of him and how much he meant to me. I wish we could have sat outside, in his sunshine, and had coffee together.

We would have finished, I'd have reached for the check, he would have grabbed it first, and I would have heard him say, "kiss my ass" one more time.

CHAPTER 3

Along with getting hired by Mr. McPatrick, being 12 brought other changes.

That summer I went away to all-boy Camp Connibuck for eight weeks on Harvey's Lake in Vermont.

Actually, it was my second summer at Camp Connibuck, but the summer I was 12 offered a distinct uptick in drama.

I had always had huge crushes on different girls.

In first grade, I remember feeling warm and nervous when we'd drive past Alice Ward's house.

In fourth grade, Connie Norman lived up the street. She was the older sister of a boy my age, a few grades ahead of us, and the most beautiful creature I'd ever seen in my life.

She had natural blond streaks in her hair and wore soft sweaters that buttoned all the way down the back.

When she got on the school bus I always looked at her and felt myself blush.

One day she sat down across the aisle from me and said, "You like me don't you?"

I felt my face get incredibly red and said, "Yes."

In the fifth grade, a gorgeous girl named Donna DelCristo

sometimes rubbed the eraser of her pencil back and forth across the back of my neck from her desk behind me and I wanted her to never stop.

Some nights I'd sleep out under the stars in the field by our house and imagine Donna DelCristo was there next to me in my sleeping bag.

I dreamed I was holding her and she was holding me.

I guess in a way I was primed for what happened at camp that summer.

Primed, but not ready.

The kids in the next tent were 13, a full year older.

One night I heard hollering and whooping, "Here it comes, here it comes, QUICK! Get me a towel!!!" all followed by great laughter.

This went on most nights.

"What's happening," I whispered to my tent mate, Timmy.

"They're jerking off," he said.

"What's that?"

"You pull on your pecker until it explodes," he said.

What?

"Why?"

"Because it feels good."

"Do you do that?"

"Tried it a few times, never worked that great. I don't think I'm old enough."

All day at camp we hiked, played tennis, raced canoes, swam, threw horseshoes, played badminton. I was good at that stuff, but all day long I dreaded the nights because I didn't understand what was happening all around me.

When I got home from camp after eight weeks I was crying one night in my bed when Mom came in my room. The light was out and she sat down next to me on the bed.

She sat quietly for a moment.

"Is it about your penis?" she said.

What?

How could she possibly have known that?

"Yes," I said.

She was quiet a moment longer.

"Honey, the fluid that comes out of your penis is the most wonderful liquid in the world. It's how a man and a woman make children."

"I know it, but…"

"When a man and a woman make love it's a good, happy thing."

"But it scares me to death, I don't really understand…"

"You hear things from your friends?"

"Yes. And I think about girls…"

When she spoke I could tell she was smiling.

"And you will for the rest of your life."

Now she made me smile.

"Good," I said finally, "because I can't help it."

Later, when the nuns and other Catholic kids said we'd go to hell if we had sex without being married, I told Mom. She stopped cooking, stared at me for a few seconds and said, "You won't."

Once when my parents visited me that year I went to camp, Mom played chopsticks on the piano in the dining hall and one of my friends told me she was beautiful.

That was the first I'd thought about how she might look to other people.

I only knew that when her smile and brown eyes shined on me nothing could ever be wrong in my world.

From the times she let me push the lawn mower when I was three or sell things door-to-door at 8 or 9 or ride my bike to distant towns in fourth grade, she set me free to find out that chances were worth taking and that starting over after mistakes is a part of everyday life and a great skill to have.

As a result, out on my own my bike got flat tires in the middle of nowhere. I flew over the handlebars onto my chin speeding down a steep hill miles from home. Once I began eating a box of Jujyfruits before I'd paid for it only to find I didn't have quite enough money. I had to negotiate with the candyman. I learned to function in a myriad of childhood run-ins with reality.

Mom knew stuff would happen, but she let me go anyway because she knew the lessons I picked up out in the world were things I wouldn't learn around the house.

The net of it all was confidence, and it's a parenting style that had much influence on my wife and me later on as we raised our three boys.

Of course, the corollary to Mom's laissez-faire child-rearing was responsibility.

If her trust in me ever faded, I knew I could hang up my freedom.

Because most boundaries were removed and my curiosity was rampant, I felt connected to everything and everyone around me. I knew most of the roads in a 10-mile radius from our house. I knew which gas stations had Cokes on ice and which had just tap water from the men's room. I was good friends with Mr. McPatrick at the restaurant, Jim the school bus driver, Johnny Malvacini who drove the local dumptruck, Frank the milkman, and Curt at the Tydol station, along with all the rich people whose lawns I'd be mowing in a few years and whose cars I washed.

And as if to keep this bonfire going it seemed Mom was always looking at me and saying things like, "Layng, in those blue jeans you're the cutest boy who ever lived."

When she said it, I believed it.

What I didn't realize was that the peaceful confidence she built daily in me was the polar opposite of what was going on inside of her.

One night at dinner time I walked into the kitchen.

Mom had the electric eggbeater on and was stirring something in a bowl. She was bent over crying.

Tears tumbled onto my cheeks as I got close to her.

"Mom," I said, "what's wrong?"

"I don't know, darling, I don't know…"

What I didn't know enough to know that day was that caring for me, plus the births of my four brothers and sisters, all born in the previous five years, had overwhelmed even her magnificent spirit. The five of us had become just too much for her to handle.

Even though our family economics were good, the managing of that sheer number of kids and their recent rapid-fire appearance was debilitating to her. Making it even more difficult was my dad's gone-early/home-late schedule and his general lack of interest in children.

Once when my parents were invited away for the weekend, Mom said to Dad, "What do you think we should do with the kids?"

He said, "I don't know, they're yours."

One contributor to that attitude was Dad's being an only child, unused to sharing the spotlight, and now sharing Mom's time and attention with others.

Why did a guy who wasn't wild about kids have five of them? Because he loved Mom, and along with her came her strict Catholic upbringing and the Church's stance against birth control. For all the pluses of Mom's banker father, flexibility was not one, and to-the-letter adherence to Church rules was not up for discussion. The struggle between the more relaxed aspects of Mom's nature, which had begun to flourish with my Dad, and the leftover power and will of her father had squeezed her into family responsibilities and an emotional state that was beyond her ability to cope.

Soon after the day I found her crying in the kitchen, Mom went off to a mental institution.

We were not allowed to visit.

That began a parade of live-in caregivers, both singles and couples, each of whom we drove off into their special cubbyholes of insanity.

The first was our paternal grandmother, Nana. Nana had grown up in Kentucky and it seemed to us she said "Kentucky" far more than necessary and when she did I told my brother it took at least 35 seconds for her to completely finish saying the word.

It would come out very slowly as "Ken-tuck-eeeeeeeeeeeeeeeeeee eeeeeeeeeeeeeeeeeeeeeeeeeeee."

My brother said it couldn't possibly take 35 seconds.

Then, without her knowledge, we timed her saying "Kentucky" and it did only take six seconds for her to finish.

I contended that was still way too long, and he agreed.

My sister, Anne, was only 1 year old when Mom went away, so of course she needed the most attention.

Nana was certainly not up to the job and would often just sit down on the kitchen chair and say, "Lordy me."

After two weeks, Dad took her back home to New Jersey.

A nice couple named the Coughlins moved in for a while but, never having had children themselves, quickly found the chaos of kids, including a 1-year-old, a bit more than they'd bargained for.

Each candidate, whether single or team, would start out smiling and saying they knew we were "all going to get along just fine," but a few days later they were screaming, saying they were going to "smack" us or "tell your father." Fortunately for us, Dad usually got home long after the exhausted helpers had retired and was gone in the morning before these miserable souls even knew what day it was.

The Coughlins lasted the longest. Almost three months.

For me, adding to the stress of Mom's absence was a teacher from hell.

After having very cuddly, loving teachers for four years in grade school, I now went to middle school and had Madame Poskowsky, a wicked and unhappy entity born and raised somewhere deep in the no-fun zone. To my knowledge, she never cracked a smile yet was sure she was drop-dead gorgeous. Even as a fifth-grader I knew she had a great figure. Had she let go the occasional smile, she might actually have been gorgeous. But instead, she strutted through the classroom like a well-coiffed sadist peeking imperiously over her half-glasses and summarily dumping on the quality of all our works-in-progress.

A classmate who had stayed back a few years was 13 years-old and was therefore "advanced" and in a position to know about such things, told us he knew what Madame Poskowsky's problem was.

"She needs a boyfriend," he said.

None of us could imagine how that would do a thing for her.

Without Mom to hold things together, all five of us kids felt mixed-up and rootless.

That spring my report card from Madame Poskowsky was terrible and I asked my dad not show it to Mom.

He did, but he showed her my brother's, too, so he wasn't discriminating.

Soon afterwards a letter from Mom came in the mail for me. I felt a sudden chill and didn't open it for three days because I thought it was about my rotten grades.

When I finally did open it, the letter never mentioned my report card.

Instead Mom said, "I hear from Peg Luders that you've become a good skier this winter. I'd love it if we could ski together some time. Maybe you can show me a few things. I think skiing is one of the hardest sports."

I cried when I read the letter because I needed those gentle words so badly.

The "Peg Luders" Mom mentioned in her letter was a neighbor, two houses away. Her son Jack was about my age, and in addition to taking me skiing while Mom was gone, Peg and her family had for years brought me along on other of their adventures, including boating around New England.

The summer of 1953 the Luders sailed me for the first time into the harborside village where I sit writing this now in the summer of 2016.

Bill Luders, Peg's husband, was a fabled racer, designer and builder of sailboats, including 1962 America's Cup winner *WEATHERLY*.

The Luders were athletes.

They played tennis.

They skied.

And they sailed.

Aces at all.

But at sailing, they were famous.

At the time they drew me onboard their yacht the *YOU'LL DO* and made me one of them, they raced a stunning black sloop named *STORM*.

STORM was a stripped-down, all-business racing craft with nothing visible below deck but highly varnished wooden ribs and a few orange life preservers.

The sails, the hull, and the skill of the sailors were all that mattered.

The *YOU'LL DO* was *STORM*'s tender, a comfortable 50-foot motor yacht made for sleeping, eating, travel, and cocktails.

YOU'LL DO accompanied *STORM* on the New England sailboat racing circuit.

The *YOU'LL DO* was gray and plain. Nice, but not fancy.

If I were to show you a picture of the *YOU'LL DO*, you would not swoon.

But when I woke up my first morning onboard, heard its engine murmuring beneath me, felt its steady vibrations, pulled on my shorts and socks and walked up four polished wooden steps to the sunny, open-air saloon and found Captain Harry alone in his dress khakis guiding the *YOU'LL DO* into the harbor of Watch Hill, Rhode Island, I was in love with the *YOU'LL DO* for life.

And though I had no way then of knowing just how deeply this coastal village of Watch Hill would affect my life, I was about to fall in love with it, too.

Before I even knew its name.

Set beside an ancient harbor, horseshoe-shaped and backed up against a hill that runs down the other side to the Atlantic

Ocean, Watch Hill has been a refuge for those seeking relief from the summer's heat since the time of the Niantic Indians in the 1600s.

Modern folks who study such things say that Watch Hill has its own "micro-climate."

That must be true, because I have now gone there every summer since 1964 and never wished I had air conditioning — not when I can have real air blowing across my pillow from out off the cool Atlantic Ocean or off Long Island Sound's gentle whitecaps.

Not when through my wide-open windows I can hear the waves pounding the beach at night, the clanging of the buoys at sea, and the lonesome squawk of seagulls in the morning.

But that first day, my entry into the most glorious harbor in the world had nothing to do with a search for cool weather. No, mine was strictly the luck of the draw. The luck of having the Luders for neighbors.

At the mouth of Watch Hill Harbor is a stone wall built out into the channel, a "breakwater" to keep surf from disturbing the boats moored beyond.

Looking out over the bow of the *YOU'LL DO,* I watched as the breakwater came closer and closer until it passed off to our right.

Then Captain Harry turned the big wooden tiller left.

I looked.

Suddenly, a new world opened.

Before my eyes was a stunning garden of white masts.

Behind them, the white faces of shops hugged the water's edge.

A tiny yacht club on pilings sat out in the water with colorful pennants strung across its roofline and flower boxes at each window holding red geraniums that tumbled out over their fronts.

A blizzard of white-trimmed, shingled summer houses looked out over the harbor and sprinkled down the hillside to the shoreline.

"Where are we, Captain Harry?"

"Watch Hill," he said.

"Wow…"

"Pretty good sight, huh?"

I looked everywhere at once.

"I love it."

"Yep," he said, "that seems to happen to everybody."

I could not even guess that my lifelong love affair with Watch Hill had just begun.

CHAPTER 4

That fall and winter, long months rolled by without Mom being home, until my birthday on March 24.

She was allowed to come home for the afternoon.

No one knew ahead of time that she was coming or I wouldn't have had a party.

As it was, an excited mob of boys were there for baseball in our field, and because of that I never really got a personal visit with her.

But every time I got up to bat I hoped I would really pound one and that Mom was watching.

That day was a watershed, because from then on every few weeks Mom would come home for several hours on Saturday or Sunday. At first she seemed tentative and fragile around all of us again, but gradually she relaxed, became more and more herself, and after about a year she came home for good.

From then on, we often had a woman named Peggy Lord around the house to help. She'd clean and do laundry, take care of the younger kids.

Peggy's help clearly took some pressure off Mom.

Peggy weighed a minimum of 300 pounds and we were all crazy about her. She was from Scotland and had her own unique string of phrases and folk wisdom.

We knew most of them by heart.

On questions of weather, Peggy would make pronouncements: "Sure as I'm Peggy Lord it's gonna be pritt-tee" or "Ohhh my, there's a rain a-comin'." When grilled as to the source of her certainty, Peggy would say, "Ya jus' look down Moe's Hole."

What?

Peggy would shoo us outside and point upwards.

"That's Moe's Hole," she'd say.

Our faces would tilt to the sky.

"See that?" she'd say.

With Peggy pointing to the heavens, we'd all look up...then at each other, wide-eyed, one micro-tickle from hysteria because no one could ever see what she was talking about.

Our favorite of Peggy's sayings was uttered if she suspected my brother and I were stretching the truth.

In that case, she would stop us mid-sentence and say, "Spread it thin, boys, we got a big farm."

My brother and I still use that one.

Mom's return slowly eased our home life back to normal.

A sure sign that the good old days were back was the first time she went around the breakfast table with a bottle of milk and poured the milk in our orange juice glasses whether or not we were finished with our orange juice.

She had done that every morning for years, and every time at least one of us had screamed, "NO, MOM! DON'T DO THAT!"

This time, it tasted just as horrible as ever, but we all glanced at each other around the table and smiled.

My brother Gene was five years younger than me and we shared a room and a set of double-decker bunk beds. At night we would talk and make up songs and poems and on weekend mornings when we wanted to sleep and one of our baby sisters would wake up early and start hysterical crying we would take turns yelling "SHUT UP!" in 30-second intervals.

Gene was very shy until he was 6 years old. When introduced to new people he would roll his eyes up into his head to make himself invisible.

Naturally, this became a source of humor to my visiting friends and they would ask to see Gene do his disappearing act.

When Mom got home from the institution she found a doctor who cured shyness in children and Saturday mornings we all piled into the car to take Gene to see Dr. Morton.

After several visits, Dr. Morton told Mom to buy Gene a toy gun.

Exactly how that would help was a mystery to all of us.

But Mom bought Gene a cap pistol and pretty soon he looked new people in the eye. A lot of my friends who came to visit were disappointed when they found out he was fixed.

Until he got braces, Gene's front teeth stuck out a bit, and even though they weren't serious "buckteeth" they were enough to earn him the name "Fang" from me.

It's only recently that our adult boys found out that "Fang" is not his actual name and that he is "Gene" to everyone but us.

Growing up, I would try out all my wrestling moves on Fang until he started crying.

Once, when I was chasing him down the driveway, I threw a car tire over his head in a perfect ringer. His legs suddenly unable to move, Fang dove headlong into the gravel driveway and cut open his scalp, launching a race to the Mount Kisco emergency room where, clothes covered in blood, he got 12 stitches.

I bought boxing gloves and forced Fang to box with me which at one point prompted him to say, "Layng, when I grow up I'm going to kill you!"

I certainly had it coming.

Eventually, the day came when he could kill me, so being the sensible, life-loving soul that I am I told him I didn't think we should fight anymore.

Now, of course, we would die for each other.

Soon after her return home, Mom began writing again, this time short stories and a column for *Family Circle Magazine* called "Teen Scene," which she wrote under the pen name "Betsy Bourne."

Her short stories were romantic and "family" in nature and were at times in most every famous magazine of the day: *Redbook, Ladies' Home Journal, The Saturday Evening Post, House Beautiful,* etc.. She often referred to her work as "Come To Realize" stories, where at the end of a traumatic experience the main character would "come to realize" some essential truth about her life.

Sometimes when Mom got paid for a story she would slip out to find "treats" in celebration and she'd surprise each one of us with something special. On one of those days she came home with five or six signs to go on the trunks of the trees in which I had built my two tree huts: "STAY OUT" "NO TRESPASSING" "PRIVATE PRO-PERTY" "MAD DOG" "TOWZONE" "NO HUNTING." I ham-mered them up everywhere and felt extremely adult and invincible when I stepped back to see the very bossy, authoritative warnings.

Mom's boss at *Family Circle,* the editor "Mr. Endicott," rose to ogre-status in her mind because his name was synonymous with the deadline for her column.

Her column was often late.

Close to deadline, if she ever thought the ringing phone might be Mr. Endicott, she'd ask someone else to answer.

More than once, when she was seriously overdue with a column, she'd ask me to ride that night with her into New York City to deliver the column by hand.

Those trips were a great adventure to me. I loved the lights and the dark and the tall buildings and all the honking traffic.

When we got to *Family Circle*'s office building in The City she'd say, "Layng, please take this up to the 12th floor to Mr. Endicott, I'll drive around the block and meet you back here."

She always said it as though it was the first time we'd ever done this, but I knew the routine by heart.

I'd go into the deserted lobby of the fancy building, punch the "UP" elevator button and hit "12" when the elevator door opened.

Since it was usually 8 or 9 p.m. when we got there, no receptionist was on duty on "12" when the elevator stopped, so I'd walk past the empty desk down the hall to Mr. Endicott's big office and knock on the frame of his open door.

Mr. Endicott was always alone, tie undone, no jacket.

His desk was huge.

He'd look up and smile when he saw me.

"Hello, Layng...had a feeling I'd see you tonight, got a column for me?"

"Yes, sir."

"Thank you. Mom in the car?"

"Yes, going around the block."

"Well, please tell her thanks, too."

"Yes sir, I will."

The year I was 12 he asked for my exact birthday and wrote it down, but I'm not sure I ever got a card from him.

Naturally Mr. Endicott seemed in no way scary to me and Mom was always a bit baffled when I returned to the car with reports of a smiling and chummy Mr. Endicott.

Having Mom home again was something none of us ever took for granted.

1954 was a year when "teen violence" and "teen gangs" got a lot of publicity, especially in tabloids like the *New York Daily News*, so no one could miss this talk on TV or on the newsstand. Since I was still only 12, I'd see these stories and tell Mom I wanted to stay 12 forever and never be a "teenager" because from everything I read or heard, all teenagers sounded like knife-wielding killers to me.

"I'm 12. I can already do anything I want to do," I said. "I don't want to be 13."

"Not every teenager goes nuts like those kids, Layng," she'd say. "You'll be a great 13 or any other age."

Aside from passing on words of comfort like those, there were other advantages to Mom being back. Most important to me, her open mind and overriding sense of "Why not?"

Her "Try It, You Can Handle It" way of raising kids always took the lead.

One day I walked into the kitchen.

"Mom," I said, "the Yanks are playing Cleveland on Friday, can I go?"

It was an unusual request.

First, because Friday was a school day.

Second because I was 12 years old and wanted to go to the game alone and the game was in New York City.

From Connecticut.

But, last fall she had almost let me skip school and take the train 50 minutes down to Yankee Stadium by myself, though not quite.

So this year?

She looked at me.

"We'll see, Layng," she said.

Oooooooooh…could she tell by my face that I smelled a "Yes" coming on?

Inside, my heart jumped. My schoolwork? It was fine. She never thought schoolwork was the most important thing in the world anyway.

Important.

But not most important.

Being a straight-shooter was most important, that and being responsible.

That night she came in my room, sat on my bed and said, "I think you're ready for that Yankee game."

I popped up from my pillow.

"Thank you, Mom!" I said. "This is a huge game."

Well, it was a huge game to me, because the Yanks and Cleveland were both hot and I was the biggest baseball fan in America and had the autograph of every player on the Yankee roster, all secured personally outside the Yankees' locker room and written in my multicolored, flip-page autograph book.

In fact, though, it was only the 12th game of the year and not actually critical at all given the 154-game season.

Since April was still chilly, I needed to wear a coat to the game.

This was no small factor.

That winter Mom had bought me a very elaborate winter coat at a fancy store called Best & Co. The coat came down close to my knees, it had a fur collar with a doubled-breasted front that buttoned to one side and was fastened by a wide belt.

This coat looked like deep overkill to me the minute I saw it. Something you might put on a prisoner as punishment or on some rich kid who never played baseball in his life.

But my Mom said I'd need it, and she got it for me even though I was embarrassed to put it on.

"Mom," I said, "the coat is too much."

"It looks so nice on you," was all she'd say.

Fortunately, the coat was only "for good," meaning I didn't have to wear it to school. Only to church, to visit our grandparents, or when we went into The City.

That was New York City.

The day of the game, I put on my Yankee jacket.

"Where are you going in that?" asked my Mom.

"To the game."

"Oh, no, young man, you'll wear your nice coat or you're not going."

I went back to my closet, took out the fancy coat, slid my arms in the sleeves, hunched up my shoulders to adjust the thick fur collar, wrapped the double-breasted front around my waist, buttoned it, and buckled the belt.

"You look great," my Mom said.

"I feel like a moron," I said.

The game started at 1 p.m., but I got there at 11:30 a.m. to watch batting practice.

That morning when I'd stepped on the train the air was still cool, but now it was warming up and the first thing I did when I reached my seat was take off my coat.

Cleveland had big stars.

Bob Feller, Early Wynn, Bob Lemon, Hal Newhouser, Al Rosen, Larry Doby and a smart, feisty manager named Al Lopez.

That day, the Indians won 9-4. Bob Lemon beat Whitey Ford.

The game wasn't over until late afternoon. By that time my section of the stands had long since lost its sunshine and the heavy shade had brought in a chill.

The point came when I could deny it no more.

I needed my coat.

As I put it on, buttoned up the double-breasted front and tightened the belt, I looked around.

"I swear to god," I wanted to say, "I'm not like you think. I hate the coat, too. It's my mother. I'm a normal…"

As a rule, when the game ended I made a beeline for the Yankees' exit door.

But that day, I got a new idea.

"The Indians," I thought. "These guys are incredible. I've got all the Yankees, I'm going to get the Indians to sign."

Outside the Indians' locker room it was different from outside the Yankees'.

Outside the Yankees' exit door there was always a crowd.

Here?

No one was waiting.

Except me.

I stood there a few minutes. No one came out.

I began to wonder if I was at the right door.

Then, right behind me, I saw a big Carey Bus.

It was idling.

"That's their bus," I thought.

The first guy out the door was manager Al Lopez.

He was a jovial-looking guy.

"Al," I said, "would you sign my book?"

He stopped.

"You want my autograph?"

"Yes," I said.

"I'm the manager," he said, smiling.

"I know," I said, "you're good."

"I'm good, huh," he said, looking at the big belt around my waist, "that's quite a coat you got on."

I looked down at the coat and felt my face get flushed.

"My mother made me wear it."

He chuckled.

"What are you, a rich kid?"

"Rich kid,"... of all the horrible things he could say.

"No," I said, "I just love baseball."

"That's good," he said, "that's good."

He took the book from my hand and wrote his name.

"Here you go," he said, and handed it back.

"Thank you," I said.

"You waiting for my guys?"

"Yes."

"Do me a favor, don't go to 'em when they walk out. Wait til they're all on the bus and I'll let you inside there for a few minutes. You can get everybody at once."

"Really? You'll do that?"

"Yeah," he said.

He took a few steps toward the bus and turned around.

The smile popped back on his face. He pointed at my coat.

"You gonna be warm enough?" he said.

We both laughed. But mine was a nervous laugh.

I wasn't used to not approaching these guys when they came out. You can't get an autograph if you don't go up and ask for it.

Suddenly, the door in front of me opened.

Bob Feller walked out.

"Holy cow," I thought.

He's so famous.

He looks just like the baseball card.

Can I just stand here and let him walk by? He's two feet from me. Nobody ever stopped me from walking right up to the Yankees.

I let him pass. His eyes straight ahead.

Wow.

The door to the bus opened. He got on.

The door closed.

"This is hard," I thought.

Boom, I heard a hand smack the locker room door and out came Al Rosen, Early Wynn and Larry Doby.

They were talking, laughing, joking back and forth.

They never looked my way.

The bus door opened, they got on and the door shut behind them.

"Geez," I thought, "I can't believe I'm just standing here. What if he doesn't let me in there?"

Soon the players were streaming past, one star after another: Hal Newhouser, Luke Easter, Jim Hegan...until Mike Garcia walked out last, stepped inside the bus, the door closed, and the team was locked inside.

What?

I can't believe I just stood there! I could've touched every one of them and I never even tried to get one guy to sign.

What a jerk.

From three feet away, I stared at the door of the bus. The engine bubbled quietly in the rear.

I paced around.

What are they doing?

Did Al forget about me?

Does he see me? Should I knock?

He seemed genuine, like he meant what he said.

"You fell for it," I thought, "god, I mean last year you chased Satchel Paige for three blocks and today you let 25 guys walk right past you."

The sun was behind the stadium now.

I was cold.

I pushed my collar up around my neck a little and wondered if I'd been put off and fooled.

All of a sudden, in a loud FLAPPP! the big tall folding door I'd been watching flew open.

Al Lopez stepped down onto the sidewalk and looked over at me.

"Hey, Rockefeller," he said, "get on the bus."

CHAPTER 5

Gradually, our rural neighborhood, long populated by people like our family and other everyday folks, was becoming kind of fancy.

As the country got more prosperous after the war, wealthy people from New York began to buy homes and weekend houses all around us. Suddenly up and down our country roads were famous people from all walks of life: Broadway producer Joshua Logan ("South Pacific"); Richard Gelb, CEO of Clairol and later of Bristol-Myers; Peter Goldmark, inventor of the long-playing record; Arthur Hays Sulzberger, owner and publisher of *The New York Times*; Vivian Vance who played Ethel Mertz on "I Love Lucy"; ex-heavyweight champ Gene Tunney and so on.

And, as much as I did not want to become a teenager, I did. It turned out there were benefits to that because along with my rising age something else went up. My earning power.

Now that there was money around our neighborhood, many of these new neighbors wanted somebody else to mow their lawns, wash their cars, and clean their swimming pools.

So began a new era for me.

The newest of these newcomers had just moved into our neighborhood.

I walked up to their classic New England home, stone wall in front, pachysandra along the elegant white-graveled driveway, ancient rhododendrons billowing up against the house, three-car garage.

I knocked on the door.

A beautiful older woman opened it wielding a big smile and holding a half-knit sweater and knitting needles.

"Hi," she said.

"Hi," I said, "I'm Layng Martine, I live down the street and wondered if you'd like me to mow your lawn this summer? I have my own mower and I also do weeding, wash cars and about anything else you might need."

She thought about that for a second or two.

"Well, come in, Layng, and let's talk about this."

"Thank you."

I stepped inside and followed her.

"I'm Alice Goodman," she said, looking back toward me. "We just moved here from The City."

We walked through the library, past an old desk, reading lamp, shelves filled with books and into the living room where she motioned me to a big soft chair opposite her couch.

"Tell me about yourself, Layng," she said.

Something in her way made me feel like telling her anything she wanted to know.

"Well, I do a lot of lawns around here. I bought my own Toro mower last year and I like the work. Toro's a great mower, you know, and it's a rotary so when I'm through you won't have any dandelions sticking up."

"Really?" she said. She seemed surprised and engaged.

"Really. They're gone."

"How old are you, Layng?"

"Thirteen."

"Pretty young to be such a go-getter."

"Lot of stuff I need and I like to be independent."

"How much are you going to charge me?"

"Well, I guess I need to see the whole lawn. May I look out back?"

We walked out across a stone patio. There was a swimming pool off to the right, a pool house, a large yard behind that with apple trees and another stone wall with an opening that led back to still another yard and a small pond.

We walked over it all.

"This will be my biggest yard," I said.

"Well, I can't say I'm surprised." There was that smile again.

"Six dollars," I said. It was hard to say "six dollars" because up til then the most I'd ever charged was three.

"Six dollars. Well, Mr. Goodman's not here, but I'm going to tell him I've found someone to take care of our yard this summer."

I beamed. I couldn't help it. I was excited to have this new job and this woman made me want to beam anyway.

And I hadn't even met Mr. Goodman yet.

As it turned out, Mr. Goodman, Benny Goodman, was famous. Very famous. Especially to the people who were my parents' age, but famous to just about everybody else, too.

Lucky for me, the Goodmans had only daughters. No sons. No built-in competition for the yard. No budding legacy to grow up and bounce me out of my top moneymaker.

But mowing the yard was just a small part of it.

I couldn't know what was around the corner.

The first time I pulled my mower up to the Goodman's when Mr. Goodman was home, he was out in the driveway walking around his gray Mercedes convertible. Red leather seats. Top down.

He heard me dragging my mower uphill through the gravel and turned around.

"Hi," I said, "I'm Layng."

He looked pretty tall to me and he was wearing round horn-rimmed glasses and the trademark Goodman smile.

"You're the kid who's gonna mow the lawn."

"Yes, sir. This'll be my third week."

"Looks pretty good."

"Thank you."

"What else do you do?"

"Well, about anything really, except mechanical stuff."

"Can you clean a pool?"

"Probably. If you show me how."

"Hell, I can't show you how, but we'll get somebody to show you."

"I'll do it."

That first morning I went to the Goodmans after Mr. Goodman got home, the sun was shining, the bees were buzzing, and when I first heard music I stopped weeding the garden.

Kneeling in a bed of roses, I listened.

From an open window, across the tops of the apple trees came the sound of a person playing the clarinet.

Up and down the scale he played.

Like a beginner.

Over and over.

Without even realizing it, I filed away the fact that the world's most famous clarinetist still practiced.

Every day.

I also filed away the fact that some weekday afternoons when my dad and most other men were off working, Mr. Goodman was sitting in a terrycloth robe by his swimming pool asleep in the sun.

This looked like freedom to me.

The first two times I mowed the Goodman's lawn, Alice Goodman put a Coke on the picnic table under the apple trees and pointed toward me and then toward it. She did it again this time, too. And she did it every week all summer. One day she and Mr. Goodman came and sat down with me and we had a talk. I knew he was gone a lot so I asked him where he'd been lately.

"Japan," he said. "Too far."

"But everybody knows you there, don't they."

He laughed. "Well, some people do."

"That's pretty amazing, go around the world and everybody knows who you are."

"Well," he said, "I guess that is a good thing."

"I want to go places," I said.

"Where would you go?"

"Everywhere."

"You'll do it," he said, "I'll bet on you."

That summer was magic to me. I did everything I could for the Goodmans. I washed and waxed their cars, cleaned the pool, swept the pool deck, weeded the gardens and, of course, cut the grass.

One night that next winter Mr. Goodman called me up and said they'd made a movie of his life and he just got a copy of it in the mail. Did I want to come over and watch it with him? We watched it in the pool house. He made popcorn. When it was over he said, "That was pretty good, wasn't it?"

"Pretty good?" I said. "That was just incredible. Is that all true?"

"Most of it."

Walking home that night in the dark, through the backyards and trails, I was especially glad Mr. Goodman didn't have a son because this way he calls on me for some of this good stuff and I get to feel sort of like his kid anyway.

One Thanksgiving when I was home from boarding school he invited me and a friend and my mom and dad to a small party. In the pool house.

"We're gonna play some music," he said.

I won't forget that night because Jimmy Rushing, the great Jazz singer, sat on a chair by the piano and he was so short his feet never touched the floor. All night he belted out his bluesy jazz and his little feet swung back and forth. The great Mel Powell was there on piano down from Yale, taking a break from the avante-electronic music he was caught up in.

After a few years, I began to feel like part of the Goodman family. Their trust and affection had become a big part of my life.

But then, a moment came when I thought I'd lost it.

It was the Fourth of July and I was just 16. Mr. Goodman was having a dinner party around the pool and I'd been preparing the yard and grounds for several days. Had to be perfect. Now the evening was upon us. The flower beds were weeded, the grass cut, the pool deck swept, the summer furniture arranged in casual groups for talking and enjoying hors d'oeuvres. The last thing of all was to vacuum the pool.

It was dusk and the pool lights were on and as I drew up the last patch of dirt the pool glowed a warm white-blue and the pristine water shimmered.

I walked around behind the pool house to shut off the vacuum system.

But, as I turned the switch, a new sound became audible.

One I'd never heard before.

It was a very powerful sound.

It slowly dawned on me that I'd accidentally hit reverse and this huge motor near me had begun blowing all the soot and dirt I'd just vacuumed out of the pool right back into the pool. By the time I got my act together it was way too late. The pool was black. The muted glow of the buried pool lights barely able to fight its way to the surface.

I moved closer.

"God," I said, horrified and fascinated by what I'd done.

I looked at my watch. People were coming in 20 minutes.

I looked at the pool. B-L-A-C-K. No change. Nothing settling.

"He'll die."

I walked toward the house. I knew Mr. Goodman was up there dressing for the night. I knew he'd had this planned for two months, that famous people were coming from everywhere, and that the last he saw of his pool 10 minutes ago it was worthy of the Beverly Hills Hotel.

I got to the screen door and called in.

"Mr. Goodman?"

Pause.

Through the screen I saw him come to the top of the stairs.

"Layng, what's up?"

"Could you come down a minute?"

"Be down as soon as I get dressed."

"Well...OK."

"Should I come now?"

"It might be better."

I moved back from the door and heard him hustle down the stairs.

"What's up?"

"I messed up your pool."

"What do you mean?"

"I'll show you."

As we walked, the pool came into view.

He stopped. Looked at me.

"What's that?"

"Dirt."

"What the hell happened?"

"I reversed it by accident and shot all the dirt back into the pool."

"Jeee-sus Christ."

"I'm sorry."

He looked at me.

"We gotta get that out of there."

"I don't know how we can until it settles."

"Settles?" he said, "you mean tomorrow?"

"Probably."

"Jesus. We've got to call somebody."

"Not sure what they could do."

A very long pause.

"You're right," he said.

He looked around. He looked at the pool chairs, the floodlights on the garden and the trees, the white-coated bartender lighting the small candles on each table, the bottles and glasses glistening under the striped awning.

"People will be here in a few minutes," he said.

"I know."

He drew a deep breath, his face relaxed and he looked at me.

"Layng," he said, "You know what I think?"

"What?"

"I think people will laugh their asses off when they see this."

I looked up at him.

"Well...I hope so..."

"They will," he said, "they'll fall all over themselves. It'll be a great party."

My heartbeat began to drop back to normal.

My face began to cool.

He put his hand on my shoulder and smiled.

"I better get inside and comb my hair."

*   *   *

Later that summer I drove Mr. Goodman in his Mercedes with the top down to a field outside Springfield, Mass., where he gave a knockout concert in a huge tent. He had a fantastic female singer with him that night. I wish I could remember her name.

At the first few notes of each song a wild blast of applause erupted and shouts of "Ben-neeeeeeeeeeeeeee!" shot up from the crowd.

Mr. Goodman leaned back and wailed.

When it was all over, men in suits and ties and women in beautiful clothes stood on their seats and clapped and screamed.

Backstage, fans, local promoters and dignitaries mobbed him.

He chatted and signed autographs. He listened to admirers' stories of how his music and their lives ran parallel, of how their first date was at one of his concerts at this or that ballroom, how they remember where they were when they first heard "Stompin' At The Savoy" or "Sing, Sing, Sing."

And then, while the heat was still on, he looked over at me and wiggled his bushy eyebrows.

That was our "high sign."

I walked outside to the car, started it and drove to the open flap of the tent.

In a few minutes he came out, got in and laid his clarinet case gently on the backseat.

We pulled slowly through the grassy field, merging with lines of cars waiting to exit, then out onto the highway.

Away from the city, the clear sky got huge and dark and the stars popped out like backlit diamonds.

After a few minutes, Mr. Goodman pushed back in his seat and I heard him exhale.

He closed his eyes.

"Hey," he said, "let's get a hot dog somewhere."

*   *   *

A few months ago my Mom died and Benny's daughter Rachel called me. We'd been childhood friends.

Some days growing up we'd sit by her pool and talk about girlfriends and boyfriends and dissect songs like Frankie Lymon's "Why Do Fools Fall in Love?"

I taught her to drive, in her family's little Karmann Ghia.

The day she called, we talked a long time and I told her some of my memories of her dad.

"Layng," she said, "I never saw that side of him."

"Of course not," I said laughing. "You're his kid. He didn't have to be a parent with me."

Rachel laughed, too, because she's been a parent.

"I guess you're right," she said.

"You know," I said, "I never called him Benny."

She took that in.

"You know, Layng," she said, "I bet he would've loved it if you had."

CHAPTER 6

During my years working for the Goodmans, Dad was advancing in his work and one winter he and Mom decided to take the oldest three of us to Florida for six weeks. Dad said he would come for a couple of weeks and Mom and the rest of us would stay down there by ourselves, the three kids enrolling in the public school as "guest students."

To the lucky three who were making this trip it sounded like a grand vacation.

But that was before we found out we were "Yankees."

No relation to Mickey Mantle, Phil Rizzuto or Yogi Berra.

It was also before we understood how devastating the Civil War had been to so many people.

In 1956 Delray Beach, Florida, our particular brand of "Yankees" were bad guys from the North to be insulted, spit on, and deprived of their bicycles and any form of friendship.

Apparently, our impending arrival had been pre-announced.

The first day I hopped off my bike at Delray's Junior High, two or three beefy seventh-graders, each of whom could've flattened my entire family just by flexing their forearms, hung out the open ground floor window, spit at me, and hollered, "Yank! You nothin'!" as I searched for a wheel slot in the bike rack.

Not that my search was worth the effort, since my bike was stolen and gone forever by lunch break.

I think the only reason I wasn't punched-out in class that first morning is that several of the larger, more threatening members of my new homeroom fell asleep during the entire a.m. session.

School days improved only slightly after the second day of recess baseball when my lead tormentor was on the mound and I managed to bury two of his pitches in the dunes beyond the outfield.

Neither time crossing home plate after these home runs did any of my teammates congratulate me or acknowledge that they had ever seen me before.

The plus side of our six weeks in Florida was the beach and the unfettered freedom in a new place.

Dad rented me another bike and we bought a big lock.

Every day after school I raced to the beach, stopping briefly at Love's Rexall Drug to get a soft, beautiful package of Charms jellied candies. Charms were like Chuckles only with no licorice, just sweet, chewy, gloriously fruity flavors. No afternoon could really start without at least one pack of Charms.

The beach was about 10 blocks from Love's Rexall and had huge, breaking rollers and a blackboard with the water temperature scrawled daily in big white chalk letters. The posting of the temperature always baffled me because who wouldn't go in the water because of the temperature?

Some days the beach was windy and occasionally my parents rented a cabana they could duck into for protection. The sand was cool inside the shady cabana and some days, if I wore myself out in the surf, I might fall asleep in there on my towel.

The tennis pro at the Delray public courts was a guy named Dick Vandenbosch. He was very handsome, smoked a pipe, and during a lesson made you feel like you were really improving while he beat the crap out of you.

Dick and his wife came over one night for drinks with my parents. During the cocktail hour my sister Sue rolled over in her bed and fell out the second floor window of our rented house, landing unhurt on the seats of our bicycles. When she walked in the front door smiling, holding her small pink "cuddly blanket" and told everyone what had happened, Dick Vandenbosch said, "Sue, you're tough. I want you on my team!"

Seven-year-old Sue puffed up like a peacock.

1956 was the year "My Prayer" was a hit by The Platters and I remember hearing that song at the tennis courts while I fell hopelessly in love with Dick Vandenbosch's tall tennis-ace daughter Sissy, who had yet to notice I existed.

Five years later I saw Sissy on spring break in Fort Lauderdale at a speech by evangelist Billy Graham.

I explained who I was and she hugged me.

I attributed that hug to Billy Graham and miracles.

Though it had nothing to do with girls or warm weather, there was one more key moment to that six weeks in Florida. It's the moment when Mom gave me a copy of Norman Vincent Peale's book *The Power of Positive Thinking for Young People.*

I lay on the living room couch and read it for several days, even when others rode off to the beach.

The book was a new awakening of sorts, clearly showing the extent to which our thoughts control our actions and therefore the course of our future.

From then on I was acutely aware of my interpretation of events, focusing on what I could DO about a problem versus focusing on how unfortunate it was that the problem had come up in the first place.

Through that book, I saw the difference between denying that bad news had occurred and recognizing bad news for what it is and looking for the next step.

60 — LAYNG MARTINE JR.

Beyond a shadow of doubt, my life was changed forever by that book.

When we got home from Florida that winter I learned that in New York State I could get a work permit at my age, 14. Since New York state was less than a mile from our house and a very busy fancy restaurant named Emily Shaw's just over the state line was looking for busboys, I got a work permit.

And a new job.

The downstairs barroom at Emily Shaw's, where I was often clearing tables, had a floor made of stone and a long woody bar.

I loved the feel of that room.

A few months ago I went back there to peek in on my old memories and found that the cozy inn where I'd worked had been recently taken over and redone by Jean-Georges Vongerichten, the tony, trendy legend of New York cuisine. At 3 o'clock in the afternoon on that day, a stunning Asian girl at a podium let me walk down the same stone steps on which I'd hustled trays as a teenager and she allowed me to hang a few minutes and soak up the old stone floor and barroom I remembered.

As I stood there and looked around, I thought of the night in that room when, in hushed tones, one of the young waiters had pointed out Kitty, the senior waitress on staff, and let on with reverence that Kitty was a force to be reckoned with and had in fact just bought a $20,000 house, a hefty amount for most anyone in those days, but an unimaginable number for someone waiting tables.

I never looked at Kitty quite the same way after that. And I can still see her face.

At home, my brothers and sisters and I were all growing into our new stages. With our increased activities and the accelerated taxiing and comings and goings, there were more demands on Mom and Dad, more emotions and moving parts than ever.

In a way, there were two families. One was me and my parents, and the other was my parents and the four other kids, all of whom were clustered together starting five years behind me in a five-year clump, and they were relatively in sync with each other.

In my early teens, by request, the small guest house Dad had built by hand years ago on our property became my living quarters, offering new independence.

In that cozy hideaway, on two head-to-head bunks, friends would spend the night, and once in a while a girl would come over and we'd get to stay in there together some afternoons and make out and no one ever bothered us. It was a situation all my pals wished they had. My parents lack of interest in micro-management meant they also had no thought of keeping beer or booze out of sight or talking up its taboos. If I was still up when they had their late dinners, wine was always offered and occasionally accepted. Our refrigerator was usually well-stocked with Piels Beer and sometimes on a hot day I'd drink one. But one day after tennis I pumped three in a row and slept for four hours, severely dimming my future interest in getting bombed.

Later, when I got to college and kids were swilling all forms of intoxicants day and night, I never quite grasped what all the fuss was about.

In ninth grade, my name began to come up frequently in my parents' family strategy sessions.

Given the age difference between me and the rest of the kids and the growing chasm between our needs and interests, and in light of my fast-developing ability to torment my siblings, Mom and Dad thought it would help things immensely if I were living somewhere even farther removed than the guest house.

So, boarding schools became a topic.

My forceful and super-Catholic grandfather was pushing for me to go to The Priory, a Catholic boys' school in Rhode Island. That idea was nixed early by my parents.

I was not an especially coveted applicant, certainly not to one of the famous boarding schools, because my academic record was middling and in no sport was I a magical athlete. My crowning achievement in junior high had been being elected "King of the School," a strictly social honor. Mom encouraged me to play that up in my application essays.

The school I got into was the right one for me, Mount Hermon School, a boys' school in northwestern Massachusetts.

Mount Hermon had strong academics, but it was earthy. Under "Crew Chiefs," the students did most all the work on campus. We cared for the grounds, did the laundry, cooked, served the food. Some of us even milked the cows on the school's farm.

Unlike at Exeter, Choate, Deerfield or Andover, few if any Mount Hermon students' dads were Fortune 500 CEOs, five-star generals or Hollywood legends. We were mostly from a solid section of America where, if there were to be any glitter, it would have to be provided by our own efforts.

Mount Hermon had been founded in 1879 by evangelist D.L. Moody of Chicago and though we went to chapel three times a week and all attended Bible class, the religious aspect of the place was evidenced more by the kindness of the professors than by any hardcore push on theology.

Many of my most important life lessons came from the men and women who taught me at Mount Hermon, long before full adulthood set in.

At one particularly vulnerable moment, I sat in my sophomore dorm room for several nights awaiting a dreaded knock on my door, hoping against hope that it would never come.

Suddenly, there it was.

I opened the door to see my dorm proctor waiting.

"Mr. Burdick would like to see you," he said.

Mr. Burdick was the school's much-loved Dean of Students.

He's the one I passed on campus a week after I arrived who said, "Coach Rineer tells me you're pretty quick on that football field."

He's the one who took me out one night onto the grass in front of our dorm and pointed to Sputnik, the tiny white dot in the sky that was the new Russian spacecraft circling the earth.

"This is history," he said. "No one's ever done this before."

He's the one I went to talk with when a boy doing pushups 10 feet from me collapsed with a brain aneurysm and never again walked or spoke a clear sentence.

And he's the one who stopped his car on homecoming weekend when I was walking with my parents, got out, introduced himself and said, "This is a great kid you've got."

But now, I knew why he'd sent for me.

It wasn't a happy reason.

"Layng?" he said when he heard a knock on his screen door.

"Yes."

"Come on in."

I walked into the homey apartment. A picture of his wife sat on the TV. He was on the couch reading the paper.

"Hi," he said, "have a seat."

"Thank you."

I chose a rocking chair.

Mr. Burdick was relaxed. He folded the newspaper and looked at me across the room.

"This may be a crazy question, but I have to ask you."

"Here it comes," I thought.

I felt so stupid.

My memory replayed the escapade I knew to be the subject of this meeting.

It was just a sunny Sunday afternoon, one of the first really nice spring days, and three of us decided to slip over to the nearby girls' school for a little excitement.

Of course, we knew this adventure was a capital crime in the eyes of the Administration.

Adding to the day's absurdity, I'd never even gotten to see my girl. Not to mention that I wasn't really that desperate to see her in the first place.

My two friends had already been caught.

The buzz all over campus was, "Did you hear Wilson and Holdredge got 'six-and-eighteen'?"

Short of expulsion, "six-and-eighteen" was the most serious punishment dished out by the school. It meant six weeks without leaving campus for any reason and 18 hours of labor done in three-hour lumps on Saturday afternoons with the school's Campus Crew.

But mostly, it was embarrassing.

"…but I have to ask you."

"Sure, anything," I said, looking back at him.

"By any chance were you with Wilson and Holdredge two Sundays ago at the girls' school?"

There was only one answer.

"Yes."

Now, here was his chance to say what a moron I was. What a dumb move I had made. How he'd had such a high opinion of me and how I'd really let him down. This was the moment for him to make it clear that the former mentor and friend and booster that he had been to me was ancient history because I was clearly not the guy he thought I was. And this was where I walk back to my room with my head down feeling more alone than ever, sure that every doubt I'd ever had about myself was true.

But I had underestimated Mr. Burdick.

Somehow he already knew that I felt stupid.

Somehow he already knew I regretted my mistake.

Somehow he knew that I was not a loser.

And somehow he didn't feel the need to say any of it.

So, after I said, "Yes," he looked at me and said, "Do you want a root beer or anything?"

*　　*　　*

Most all the professors at Mount Hermon, male and female, seemed focused on whatever was good about us and on helping us where we needed improvement.

If an academic subject or anything else gave us trouble, it was not uncommon to be invited to a professor's house in the evening for extra attention, often leading to a warm piece of pie or a few brownies made by someone in the family.

Sometimes I wonder how I would have made it without the kind words and hugs, both literal and figurative, from my Mount Hermon professors.

A lot of the professors were also coaches, and I remember how often they'd say that playing sports was great training for life. That always puzzled me because to me playing sports was so much fun. Of course later I saw what they were talking about. I saw that I could start out way ahead in a game, or in life, and fall far behind in a heartbeat, and I saw beyond question that if I fell far behind in something I could still end up a winner.

I suppose my coaches had always been spouting that wisdom, but I credit Mount Hermon with pinning this priceless information permanently to my brain.

As onerous as Mount Hermon's "Work Program" sounded to friends whose schools were without such a thing, in my three years there I liked every assignment I ever got, especially the ones requiring me to work by myself. Alone, I could do the job the way I wanted to do it and, while working, my imagination could float off to anywhere uninterrupted.

My first year, I steamed garbage cans back behind the kitchen, and one spring I was the guy who raked the base paths on the baseball diamond and sculpted the pitcher's mound. In both cases I worked solo. My work on the diamond was done at dawn. I loved the silence, the privacy. And I loved the look of it when I was finished and the sun rose and lit up the neat new lines my rake had made.

The room dedicated to garbage-can steaming had excellent acoustics and even when the steamer was on full blast, if I sang

"Hound Dog" or "Peggy Sue" the echo provided by the brick walls and the cement ceiling convinced me I was minutes from stardom.

In fact, the one time I tried singing with a band, at a dance held jointly with our nearby girls' school, a few girls screamed when I started and continued on until they realized I only knew the words to the chorus, at which point they found something else to talk about.

And though music remained my preferred form of culture as a teenager, I soon came across a book that has helped me for 48 years.

That book today would look like a most primitive version of the now-ubiquitous flood of "how to" real estate books.

My prime takeaway from this book was that if I could come up with the cash for the down payment on a house, then rent it out, the rents I received would pay it off for me.

This new and beautiful concept seemed related to the "freedom" I was after and made such simple sense to me that it went in my head and stayed there forever.

Years later, when married, not only was the first house we owned a duplex (a two-family house) with our tenant's rent making most of our mortgage payment, but so was our second house, followed by a number of other properties I bought and sold to stay afloat while attempting to make a living in what I eventually found to be my chosen profession.

Even today, we have rents coming in and I have huge respect both for my tenants and for every dollar we receive from them.

At 17 what attracted me to that early real estate book was that, even with ready cash always on hand from my various jobs and with no living expenses, occasionally cackling at me from the back of my mind was the dark thought that someday I would be a grown-up and have to do something that made enough money to actually support myself, not just to buy popsicles and baseball gloves.

That seemed a daunting and baffling task.

Senior year at Mount Hermon, when the campus talk turned to college applications, I needed advice.

My dad's alma mater, Princeton, sent an extremely handsome and likable young rep to Mount Hermon where he set up in a conference room to conduct interviews.

Much as I suspected that I was not the quality of candidate he was looking for, I signed up for an interview anyway.

As I waited outside the closed door, several friends came out reporting that the man was impressed with their grades and test scores and had all but begged them to apply to Princeton. Encouraged that Mount Hermon was on a roll that night and that it might rub off on me, I felt a brief swell of hope.

When my turn came to be interviewed, I went into the conference room and sat in a leather easy chair opposite this young, cool-looking guy and felt completely at home. But, after a 30-second scan of my qualifications, this same most-winning of people looked me in the eye and said, "Layng, I know your dad is an alum, but Princeton is not the spot for you."

Then he smiled and, as though we'd been pals for 15 years, pushed my transcript aside and asked if I was a big Red Sox fan.

Of course, I knew I was not an academic. But even our own college counselor seemed distressed by the brevity of the list he had compiled of colleges for which I might be a contender.

I went to see Mr. Burdick, Dean of Students, my wise longtime booster and go-to adult when the chips were down, the man who had said, "Do you want a root beer or anything?"

I sat down in the rocking chair where I'd been many times before.

"What's up?" he said.

"I've got to figure out a college," I said, "and my test scores and grades lack a little magic."

Mr. Burdick smiled.

I wasn't telling him anything he didn't know.

Mr. Burdick, himself a Princeton grad, put his hands behind his head and leaned back.

He looked over at me.

"On the other hand," he said with a twinkle, "I just saw the new yearbook. You got voted 'Class Lover'."

I smiled.

"Yeah," I said, "I hear every college is looking for one of those guys."

He said nothing for a minute or so and then, thinking, still smiling, he started talking.

"You know, Layng, I've seen your grades, I know all about grades and I can tell you this, you're going to get into a good college and you're smart as hell…but you've got something as good or better than grades and test scores."

Not the speech I was expecting.

"I do?"

"Yes, you do."

"And what is that?" I said.

"Spirit, Layng…you've got spirit. And it's your spirit that's going to give you a good life."

This felt so good I couldn't stand it.

"Thank you, that means everything to me."

"But you're smart as hell, too."

"You think so…"

"I'm one hundred goddam percent positive."

CHAPTER 7

I did get into a good college. Denison University in Granville, Ohio.

So, with that arrow in my quiver and my Mount Hermon diploma, I bought a $500 bright yellow 1954 Ford convertible and took a summer job I didn't want.

Selling magazines door-to-door.

Dad thought it would be "good for me" and some friend of his said he could "get me in."

I already had a job for that summer, but Dad wanted me to try this one, so I did.

Why anyone needed connections to get this job is beyond me, but that's another story.

The first day I showed up, five or six of us sat in folding chairs in front of a heavy-set guy at a desk, Mr. Kendurso.

Mr. Kendurso introduced me to his troops and assigned me to "go out" with two of them, one of whom had a car and drove. His name was Richie. Richie was the head of our "Group."

We piled into Richie's four-door Chevy.

Richie and his partner named Fez lit cigarettes and announced that our first stop would be Lou's Diner in New Canaan "for coffee."

By the time we left the diner it was 9:30 a.m.

We drove to a neighborhood pre-selected by Richie that was supposed to be "good."

So far, I had no idea what was up.

Richie parked, turned around to me in the backseat, and explained the system.

"You go house to house," he said, "knock on the door...first thing you do when they open up is give them this." He handed me a piece of paper roughly the size of a paper placemat.

"This here is a bunch of recipes. Women love this. They love recipes, and you're giving them something for nothing. They'll take it. They'll like you. Then you engage them: 'You like to cook?' 'What are your favorite foods?' 'Italian? Is your family Italian?' Then you talk about LIFE Magazine or whatever that has the Pope on the cover this week or something and you say, 'Did you know you can have LIFE Magazine delivered to your house for only 7 cents a week?' blah blah like that. What you want her to do is sign up for at least three magazines and you walk away with 'The Front'...that's the front money. Usually about a buck thirty for three magazines. Okay? That's yours. The front. Are you with me? You fill out all this here stuff for each sale — name, address, so on — bring it back to me. Go for like ten fronts a day. All right?"

He paused.

"You don't look good. Did I lose you?"

"No, no, I got it."

"Okay, so here's your packet. You go..." he looks around, points to a street, "...up there."

He consults his watch.

"It's 10 of 10. Meet back here at noon, we'll go to lunch."

Richie and Fez exit the car and stride off in another direction.

I head for my appointed street.

I knock on my first door. After what seems like a full minute of a tiny voice calling "All right, all right, all right..." a very old woman opens the door and looks through the screen.

"Yay-ysssss," she says, squinting and uncertain.

"Hi," I said, "my name is Layng Martine, I have some recipes here, for you."

"Did I order recipes?"

"No, there's no charge. They're for you."

"But, I don't cook. I haven't cooked for years. Didn't Charlotte tell you that?"

Charlotte?

"No, I'm sorry, I didn't know that."

"Charlotte," she called inside, "the recipe boy is here."

"Who the hell is that?" hollers a voice from back in the house.

"Your friend with recipes."

"Ma'am," I said...

Another woman comes to the door in a bathrobe, towel around her head and without her teeth.

"What are you selling?" she says.

"Magazines," I say.

"What's the recipe, bullshit?"

"It's a gift, it's..."

"Gift, my ass," she points at the old lady, "can't you see she don't know a dog from a biscuit? Get the fuck out of here."

The door slams shut, shade comes down.

I decided to drop the recipes.

It might work for some people, but it felt like a scam to me.

I decided to just sell the magazines.

I sold two sets of three magazines by lunch time and went back to meet the guys. I had $2.60 in my pocket. Two "fronts."

"Hey, that's good," said Richie, my Group Head, "them recipes work nice, huh?"

"I didn't use the recipes."

"No? What'd you do?"

"I told them I was selling magazines."

"No shit?"

"No shit."

"You got the fronts?"

"Yes."

"Nice. Okay, lunchtime."

I did that for two days before I quit.

My mom told me I was a "welcher."

"Mom," I said, "I tried it. I hated it. I'm not spending my summer doing that. I never wanted the job in the first place. I thanked the guy. I was polite. And, I can make three times the money doing lawns and gardens and I don't have to con anybody."

That night my friend, Bobby, called me.

"Are you home?" he said.

"Yes."

"I'm coming over. I got a great idea."

Bobby pulled in the driveway with a station wagon full of fuzzy bedroom slippers.

"Look at these things," he said, ripping open a large carton and holding up a pair of aqua-colored women's slippers.

"Where'd you get these?"

"Wholesale, a guy I know imports them from Uranus or somewhere."

"They're nice."

"I paid a buck, we can sell them for $2.50."

I looked at the slippers. They were soft and washable and came in six colors. I put a pair on and walked around.

"Door to door?" I said.

"Yes."

I looked at him.

"I'm in."

For openers, we went to a new development where the houses were close together and no trees or shrubs had yet grown to block visibility between them.

We instituted a sales method that proved to have a high charm-factor.

First, we put a different-colored slipper on each foot.

In our hands, we held another color slipper for prospective customers to touch.

That way, between the two of us, all six of our color-choices were showing.

We'd go up to houses that were side by side wearing the slippers and knock on the front doors at the same time. When the two women came to their doors, we'd point across the yards at each other and the two women would look over and see their friend.

Right away, any apprehension felt by the prospects would disappear, and most got tickled at the absurdity of two teenage boys wearing and waving women's bedroom slippers.

The women would usually call out to each other and everyone would start laughing.

Our verbal sales pitch was short and basic:

"Soft, comfortable, washable, last forever...choose from six colors, here, try these on!"

We began to call this two-women-at-once sales method "The Irresistible," because it rarely failed.

By the end of the summer we were so cocky that if we came across one of these new developments, we'd just look at each other, eyes would widen, and we'd shout, "IRRESISTIBLE!"

Too bad those side-by-side-house neighborhoods with no trees were so hard to come by, because the laughs always felt so good to everybody.

Even though it was unlikely we'd ever be back to most neighborhoods we visited, our stated goal was to make everyone happy with their purchase.

One time we sold slippers to the women on both sides of a duplex, but we didn't have the color one of the ladies wanted.

When we returned with her color, the woman on the other side of the duplex burst out her front door in a frenzy holding what looked like two jelly rolls.

"Look at these," she said, waving the item up in my face, "you call this a product? It's..."

The jelly rolls turned out to be two maroon-colored slippers that had been washed and then put in the dryer.

I smiled.

"Oh," I said, "this is my fault. Can't go in the dryer. Washer, but not dryer, and I must not have told you that. Let me run to the car and get you another pair. I'm sorry!"

Every day, we sold slippers until we'd both sold 20 pair. That usually happened by about 1 p.m. And in 1960, this schedule made us more money than we'd ever dreamed of so we decided to make use of it.

Some days, if we'd been out late the night before, we'd just go get a few hot dogs and fall asleep in a park.

But most days, we'd plot an adventure.

"I think we should go skydiving," I said one day.

We drove to Massachusetts where a small hut at an airfield offered three hours of skydiving lessons before they hooked you to a parachute and took you up in a plane to jump out.

The instruction was minimal. And suspect.

Our 28-year-old instructor, dressed in sunglasses, white combat boots and an all-white zippered bodysuit, spent the first half hour of our group "lessons" fanning his hot coffee and telling us how he almost got killed the first time he jumped and then almost died again two years later when he tried a tandem dive with his ex-wife and their bloodhound puppy.

By the time the instructor finished his coffee, two people had forfeited their $35 and left the property.

"All right," he said to the remaining seven.

"For openers, I want you guys to get up on this picnic table, jump off, and roll."

The intrepid seven stepped up on a long bench, then onto the picnic table, from which we jumped two and a half feet down to the grass and rolled, a roll which took all the energy we could muster since after the short jump we were barely moving.

"Nice," he said, "okay that's about what it's gonna feel like when you exit the plane and hit the ground in your parachute."

Bobby looked over at me.

"Is this guy for real?" he said.

In less than three hours we were airborne above the fields and farms of western Massachusetts.

We stood one behind the other inside the plane, each attached by a "static line" to a long pipe fastened to the ceiling. Each of our static lines was 300-feet long and theoretically would open the chute when we jumped out and fell 300 feet from the plane.

There was a high, wide doorway cut out of the fuselage and one by one we were supposed to get in the open door, grab handles on either side and, when the instructor tapped our forehead, jump out backwards.

The instructor had already told us that when our turn came, if we didn't go out he'd have to push us out, otherwise we'd block the others.

A German-accented woman about 50 years old was connected to the static line in front of me.

She had asked a lot of questions during the brief instruction class.

"Suppos I chain-ch my mindt and don't vant to go?" was one of her questions.

"Like I say," the instructor told her, "if you don't go by yourself, I push you out. Can't block the door for others. Your static line will open the chute."

When our plane reached altitude, a young construction worker named Frank was the first person to set up in the doorway.

Waiting my turn, the propeller blast was so loud I could barely think straight.

The instructor visually checked Frank up and down, then gave a quick tap on his forehead.

Frank launched himself backwards into the blue and disappeared.

Then the second guy went, a local high school football player.

Now, it was the German woman's turn.

She was shouting something no one could hear.

Then she stepped up to the doorway and lay down in fetal position.

The instructor bent down and shouted in her ear.

The German woman didn't move.

The instructor lifted his head and looked at the rest of us lined up to go.

He bent down again, even closer this time, and hollered.

But she just lay still.

Sensing an impasse, the instructor stood up, gently positioned the instep of his foot beneath the small of the German woman's back and flipped her out the door.

*　　*　　*

Every day that summer was a taste of freedom. Bobby and I invented our days. In retrospect, we were also inventing ourselves. We were responsible. Having fun. And under nobody's thumb. By the end of the summer we'd sold almost two thousand pair of slippers.

Some afternoons we had played tennis until darkness covered the courts and we had to quit.

Then sometimes I'd shower and treat a date to exotic drinks and nightclubs and music in New York's Greenwich Village and Harlem and on Broadway.

We'd pay too much for a cup of coffee to hear an obtuse Village folk singer or poet in a room so otherwise quiet you could hear somebody tie their shoes, then we'd go up to Small's Paradise in Harlem, a spot so loud and crowded and full of life you thought that surely everyone in the whole world must be there. At Birdland on Broadway we got our pictures taken by the fancy club photographer and the girl would take the picture home in its simple cardboard frame.

The next morning by 9 a.m. Bobby and I would be out selling slippers.

One night during dinner I got a phone call.

It was from a famous kid a few years older than me who lived in Darien, two towns away.

I say "famous" because he was famous in the way that high school legends spread around a region.

This guy's grapevine resume was that he was the handsomest guy in the galaxy and a devastatingly great athlete.

Calling me?

"Layng," he said, "this is Lee Schilling. I hear you're coming to Denison next year."

I gathered my cool.

"Lee, hi," I said, "yes, going to Denison, excited about it."

"Coach Piper says you're coming out in a few weeks for early football."

Jesus, I was trying to forget about that.

"Yes," I said, "you gonna be there?"

"Damn right. Look, I was wondering if you'd like to meet up somewhere, throw the football or something, get to know each other a little between now and then?"

This was the most important phone call of my life. But I didn't know it.

A few years later, Lee would become my brother-in-law.

But tonight, unbeknownst to me, Lee was scouting prospective new pledges for his Denison fraternity Phi Gamma Delta.

We made a date to meet at Darien High School.

I got there early and sat waiting in my convertible.

Though I'd never seen Lee before, I figured I'd spot him.

I was right.

He was unmissable.

A station wagon pulled up beside me.

There he was.

Huge smile, curly brown hair, lifeguard-tan.

All as advertised.

"You Layng?"

"Yeah, Lee, how are you?"

We got out, shook hands. In one hand, Lee palmed a well-scuffed football.

"You a running back?" he said.

"Yeah halfback, kickoffs, punt returns, you?"

"Fullback. I think you'll like the coach."

We ran each other ragged.

Lee could throw twice as far as I could and I'd be half-exhausted running out for a pass by the time he let go of the ball.

One time when he hadn't thrown after I'd run about 60 yards, I stopped and called back to him, "Lee, don't bother throwing, I'm in New Jersey!"

Lee laughed his ass off.

Finally, we both collapsed in the cool grass and lay there a few minutes looking up at the sky.

Just as my eyes were closing I heard him say, "Hey, let's get a Dairy Queen."

At the sound of ice cream, I came to life.

"Perfect," I said.

Unfortunately, standing up in our gym shorts and patting our non-existent pockets, neither of us had brought a wallet.

"Damn," he said.

Suddenly, I snapped my fingers.

"Hey," I said, "we're golden."

"Why's that?"

"Because my back seat is full of bedroom slippers. We'll sell a few pair to the girls at the Dairy Queen and get whatever we want."

"What the hell are you doing with a back seat full of bedroom slippers?"

"I sell them."

"To who?"

"Door-to-door."

"Just knock on doors?"

"Yup."

"Shit, I gotta see this."

We waited in line.

When our turn came, a pretty girl said, "Hi, may I help you?"

"Hi," I said, holding up two pair of slippers. "We don't have any money, but we have these fuzzy, very cozy bedroom slippers in six colors..."

"What?" the girl said, her smile growing.

The slippers in my hands were turquoise and maroon.

"They're very soft," I said, "make it a lot more fun to walk around in there."

I looked at the slippers and then back at her.

"Could we trade you for two shakes?"

She looked at the slippers.

She looked at me.

Her eyes got wide.

Then she broke out laughing.

"Hey, Muriel," she called to the girl at the other window, "this guy wants to trade us some bedroom slippers for ice cream!"

Muriel left her window, the two girls stopped everything, bent over, put the slippers on, tromped around giggling wildly for a minute or two then each bought a pair.

Our girl stood at the window wiggling her toes and looking down at her slippers.

"These are comfortable," she said with another big smile.

"I'm glad. They better be."

"What do you want?"

"Two vanilla shakes," I said.

"And a sundae?" she said

"A sundae? Really?"

"Yes. Muriel and I are throwing in two sundaes."

"Wow. Thank you," I said. "Okay, one hot fudge," I looked at Lee, "and one butterscotch."

We took our four treats to a cement table outside and devoured them without a word.

"Holy cow," Lee said when he finished, "I'm a blimp." Then he pushed the empty cups away, put his head down on the table and closed his eyes.

"I've got more slippers," I said, tapping him on the shoulder.

He opened his eyes and smiled.

"I'm done," he said.

Lee's phone call that summer night is still the best one I've ever gotten.

We both got so much more than a workout and those Dairy Queens.

We each got a best friend, and years later, I married his sister, who changed my life forever.

*   *   *

On the last weekend of August, my slipper-selling buddy Bobby and I got in his mom's two-tone green 1956 Chevy station wagon and decided that as a last final blowout sendoff to our summer we'd drive south until we saw a palm tree, make an immediate u-turn, head home and call it a day.

Which we did.

FYI, the first palm tree from Connecticut was in Myrtle Beach, South Carolina.

*   *   *

I had kept one week open and unbooked before I had to leave for Denison and early football.

I took my toothbrush, a clean shirt and underwear and drove my yellow convertible 10 hours to Quebec City Canada where I rented a dark, chilly room above a bar.

I was going to "write."

I had read John Updike. J.D. Salinger. John Steinbeck.

Isn't this what they did?

The bar was on the docks.

The men at the bar were rough.

It was raining and windy and the room was unheated.

Midway through the second night I got very lonesome.

I couldn't get to sleep.

I wrote nothing.

In the morning I got crepes at an all-night Belgian bistro, cranked the car and drove home, stopping only for gas and for fried clams at Howard Johnson's, where I took out the diary I had planned to fill up in Quebec City.

At the top of the first page I wrote:

SUMMER 1960

Sold bedroom slippers door to door.

I was free.

It was wonderful.

CHAPTER 8

One day back from Quebec City I flew off to early football at Denison University with no real direction.

At least, not academically or for a career path.

I knew I cared a lot about people, that I loved the camaraderie I felt with friends.

And I thought I was a good writer, several of my Mount Hermon professors had said so, too, but that was about it for any long-range clues.

On the Denison football team I excelled at singing in the shower and on the bus when we traveled, but I prayed the coach would never call my name to actually get on the field and play football because I rarely knew what I was doing and did not want to get pounded by the gigantic people on the other team.

At Denison, my "thing" was social. I had massive crushes on two successive girls and made deep friendships that have never let up. But I never dove into the academics.

I joined Lee's fraternity, loved my "brothers," and as a pledge barely noticed the inanities of "Hell Week," like standing sleepless in front of the fraternity house for 24 hours, a pellet gun in each hand "guarding" a framed picture of the fraternity president's girlfriend.

I ran varsity track as a freshman and might have been an out-standing sprinter had I remembered what I'd long ago learned selling slippers and Cloverine Salve…namely, that practice really does pump up the result.

Like Mount Hermon, Denison was a bit far away from things, so I pursued wonderfully enjoyable but wasteful adventures like hitchhiking 1000 miles to Brown University in Providence, Rhode Island, to visit friends for a "long weekend" (five days) and for the hum of a city.

I did manage an "A" on one paper. A research treatise on Benny Goodman called "Licorice Stick," the hipsters' term-of-the-moment for a clarinet.

But when the grades came in, my dad had the good sense to tell the school I would not be back for sophomore year. At least, not on his dime.

It was a good call because my report card was barely breathing and he was not getting his money's worth.

Considering that I lived at Ray Charles concerts and rock 'n' roll clubs, never changed my bedsheets once in nine months and only owned books for four of my five classes, I wasn't getting his money's worth either.

So, instead of going to college for my sophomore year and in one of Dad's best moves ever, because of my apparent "writer" interest he used his connections to get me a job somewhat related to writing. In New York.

The intent was to take a year off from school and get a taste of the real world, grow up, see if anything stuck. Maybe come up with a game plan.

So, in July 1961 I became a copyboy at TIME magazine. This simple job pushed me to new clues about myself. Every day I was surrounded by brilliant writers like Calvin Trillin, John McPhee and John Gregory Dunne, all of whom went on to become famous authors.

But back then, they wrote the most important news stories of the day for TIME.

Sometimes the writers would suggest books for me to read. I'd read them. When an event of the day puzzled me or I needed background on it, I'd ask and they'd fill me in.

My curiosity was constantly up and constantly satisfied.

Long before the internet, TIME had a bank of telex machines at the end of the hall that would yield the most obscure fact or detail within minutes. Khrushchev's ring size? Coming up. Joe DiMaggio's first coach? No problem.

I devoured every minute I was there.

As a copyboy, I made and delivered the TIME writers' coffee.

I sharpened their pencils.

When they buzzed me, I brought their stories to the editor. And on special occasions, when there was something important to watch, I set up folding chairs for them in front of the TV in the Senior Editor's office.

I didn't do this for all the writers. Just the ones in "The Nation" section, the very first section of the magazine. Our section was focused on domestic issues.

My job was absolutely critical to the orderly operation and enjoyment of daily life for all those under my care. They couldn't do without me.

Or so I thought, and the need to do this job well consumed me.

Then, one day my devotion to it nearly did me in.

In fact, had a camera been on me, I doubt anyone would have hired me ever again for anything.

I was commuting to work by train from my parents' home in Connecticut to New York City.

It was a sunny weekday morning when I leaped out of my road-worn convertible at the Greenwich railroad station.

"This is the 7:25 train to New York...next stop, Grand Central, all aboard!" I heard the station master's announcement as I raced across the parking lot.

I saw the train.

Not yet moving.

I flew up the stairs and through the overpass hoping for a miracle.

As I hit the top of the staircase the train began to squeak forward.

I scrambled downward and reached the platform in time to see the silver cars slipping away.

Faster. Faster.

Through the moving windows I saw people settling into their seats.

I stopped cold.

And it was gone.

"Jesus."

My job. They'll fire me.

It was February 20, 1962.

Missing the train on this day was especially unacceptable because it was a day they might shoot astronaut John Glenn into space.

Although, they might not shoot him into space.

Everything hinged on the "countdown."

For a few days now there had been a countdown, but for one reason or another it had never reached "Lift-off."

The countdown was to resume this morning.

There was great excitement. Great apprehension. Everyone was glued to it.

Especially "my" writers in "The Nation."

If there were no sharp pencils, no coffee, no folding chairs set up in front of the TV what would they do?

The next train was in 25 minutes. And it was a local.

Very slow, many stops.

No chance to make it by 9:00.

I wouldn't be there to prepare things, to deliver steaming brew in their favorite cups, arrange neat chair rows for those who would chronicle the biggest event of the day for the world's greatest weekly news magazine.

My mind jumped to the one alternative to the train.

My car.

Oh, but that was impossible.

It had no brakes.

Well, it had brakes but they didn't work.

Well, they worked but you only got three pumps before the pedal went to the floorboard.

Then you had to fill up the master cylinder with brake fluid to get another three pumps.

Yes, the fill-up hole for the fluid was handy, right there under my knees, but driving-and-filling, driving-and-filling was not easy. And it felt very risky for the 25-mile drive into The City.

But what was my choice? Lose my job? Let everyone down? They'd told me this whole year I was the best copy boy ever. The idea of not being that anymore was…unacceptable.

I ran to my car, turned the key and made a plan.

I would stay at least five car lengths behind the guy in front of me.

I would not speed. I would stay in the right-hand lane.

I would take it easy, steadily knock out the 25 miles and get to the TIME-LIFE building before anyone even missed me.

Navigating the first toll booth went smoothly.

I approached slowly, tapped the breaks twice, did a slow roll up to the basket and fired in my quarter.

Green light!!

So far so good.

Accelerate gradually up to speed.

The traffic moved in an easy flow. Lots of space.

I hung back. Very conservative.

Occasionally I would shoot a glance over at the box of brake fluid on the passenger seat and feel comfort.

One can was open, held firmly between my legs.

On a lengthy straightaway I replenished what my two taps at the toll booth had depleted.

Good system.

Small swell of confidence.

Radio?

Why not.

I clicked it on and heard the end of "Great Balls of Fire."

The ride was taking on an air of normalcy, predictability.

I looked at my watch. 7:47.

Train I missed can't be doing too much better than this.

The road wound through wooded Westchester and soon entered the urban outskirts.

I could feel the city getting closer.

Geez, I'm gonna make it.

Up ahead, no cars were even visible in my lane.

That is, until I rounded a corner and saw that ahead of me a line of several hundred cars was at a dead stop.

I jammed three hard pumps down on the brake pedal before it flew quickly to the floor.

I surveyed ahead then reached for the brake fluid between my legs, aimed it into the hole in the floor and poured.

Overflow spread everywhere.

Three more pumps, slower but still moving.

Reached for another can from the box beside me. The small white Volvo in my lane ahead wasn't moving.

I'm closing in on it fast.

I tried to open a new can and steer.

There is no way I can help hitting the Volvo.

I knew I was going to hit it at least 10 seconds before I slammed into it and folded it up into a shape similar to an upside down "V."

During that 10 seconds I thought how amazing it was that I was going to hit him, and that I hadn't hit him yet, but I was going to and I knew it but he didn't.

The crash came as a complete shock to the man in the Volvo.

When he forced open his crumpled, squeaking door and climbed down onto the road, his horn rimmed glasses were hanging off one ear and he was shaking his hands in a fury.

"I'm a father!!! I have a family!!!"

He stomped, he swore, he pounded on the hood of my car.

"Why did you do this!!!"

I remember that I had on a yellow sweater and how I wished it were brown, or maybe just a simple blue shirt.

"I'm sorry," I said, "I couldn't stop."

"Couldn't stop? You could've killed me!!"

He was right. I felt incredibly guilty.

I thought of the box of brake fluid on the front seat.

A State Trooper appeared.

The Volvo's driver ran up in front of him and hollered, "This guy tried to kill me!!"

The trooper looked past him.

"Who's car is this?"

"Mine," I said.

"Who's car is this?" he said, pointing to a Chrysler now joined to the front of the Volvo.

"Mine," said a tall man in an overcoat.

"Are you all right?" the trooper asked him.

"Yeah. My seat's off the track, but…"

"I should be a dead man!" the Volvo's driver shouted, "I'm alive by the Grace of God!!"

The trooper looked at him.

"What are you gonna do to him?" the driver demanded.

"I'm going to find out what happened first."

"What happened? He drove into me going 75 miles an hour, that's what happened! Look at my car!"

"Sir," the trooper said, "I will take a statement from everybody."

"I won't stand for this!"

"Sir, I'll have to ask you to calm down. We have a procedure and I'll get to you."

"Procedure, my ass, this guy's a goddam criminal!!!"

With that, he pounded hard again on the hood of my car.

Something changed in the trooper's appearance.

"Sir, you'll have to come with me," he said, and put his large hand on the smaller man's shoulder.

"Me?"

"Yes, sir."

"I'm on my way to work, he almost kills me, and you're giving me a hard time?"

The trooper was finished talking.

He moved the man by gentle force across the median, opened the back door of his police car, put the man in and closed the door.

The man hollered. But we couldn't hear him anymore. He slammed his fist repeatedly against the window, his face contorted. He tried to open the door.

But there were no door handles on the inside and he couldn't get out.

The trooper looked at me.

"What happened?"

"I came around the corner, traffic was dead-stopped, I couldn't stop in time and ran into this white car."

He looked at the tall man in the overcoat.

"What happened?"

"I was stopped, next thing I knew I got whacked from behind."

"All right, I need to see both licenses and registrations."

I went back to my car.

From the passenger side I slid the box of brake fluid onto the back floorboards, put the two empty cans in there, closed the top of the box and took my registration from the glove compartment.

The trooper took down all our information, closed his report book, and looked at me.

"Need a wrecker?"

"I don't think so. One fender is bent in against the wheel but I think I can pull it away."

He walked over to my car.

It was a 1955 Buick with those huge chrome "breasts" for bumpers and, considering the damage caused, the car looked pretty good.

The trooper looked at the fender.

"Grab a hold of this over there," he said.

Together we tugged and slowly pulled the fender out from the wheel.

We rested for a few seconds, then bent down and moved it back a little more.

The trooper stood up to look.

"I think that's gonna do it."

"I think you're right. Thank you. I couldn't have done that by myself..."

"You know you were lucky today."

"Yes, sir, I do."

"Watch what the hell you're doing will you?"

"Yes, sir."

He turned and walked back toward the man in the overcoat.

I got back in my car and looked at my watch.

8:26.

I can still make it.

Just then, in front of me, a tow truck eased up to the rear of the Volvo.

It hooked onto the Volvo's rear bumper and lifted.

The tow truck driver got out to check the connection, climbed back into the truck, revved his engine, and in a festival of sparks from the Volvo's dragging front bumper, hauled the car off to the junkyard.

Across the median, locked in the back of the police cruiser, I saw the Volvo's owner.

He was hammering his hand against the window and screaming.

But no one could hear him.

Directly ahead, the trooper and the tall man in the overcoat seemed to be bonding over the tall man's Yankee baseball cap, which he now held in his hand and was pointing to.

I checked my rearview mirror and waited for a break in the traffic.

Soon I saw one, slipped into it, and headed off toward The City.

By the time I got to Sixth Avenue in Manhattan I was three blocks from my office and all the parking spaces were taken.

Except for one by a fire hydrant.

Under the circumstances, the threat of a $50 parking ticket didn't faze me.

I backed into the spot, got out and started running.

Clocks must have stopped for the past hour and a half.

On the 25th floor of the TIME-LIFE Building I was the first one to arrive in "The Nation."

In no time I had the coffee started, the TV turned on, and the folding chairs set up.

I laid a yellow pad and sharp pencil on each seat.

A large closeup of the huge white rocket took up the TV screen and the commentary and countdown was running..."T-Minus 63" showed in the corner of the screen.

Sixty-three minutes till lift-off.

Writers soon drifted in, one at a time, glanced at the TV, went to their offices.

I brought them coffee.

"Looks like he may go today," I said.

"Could be."

The count continued. T-minus 22.

By 10 o'clock, everyone was gathered in front of the TV and paying attention.

"No false start today," Lea South said. There had been five. She tapped her sharp pencil on the edge of her pad.

Sometime before 11am John Glenn was fired up into space and became the first American to orbit the earth.

About 2 p.m. I was sent over to The Associated Press to get the first photographs.

Down the elevator, out the front door, about to race across Sixth Avenue to Rockefeller Center and the Associated Press offices.

But, I couldn't cross.

Traffic was bumper to bumper and no one was moving.

I'd never seen this before.

What's going on?

I looked over the sea of stopped cars. Up about three blocks fire engines were clustered, set at hurried angles. Red lights blinked. A tall ladder sprang from the rear of one truck, leaned against a four-story building and a fireman was climbing.

Since my mission was temporarily impossible, I ambled up the sidewalk toward the action.

When I got in front of the building, a thick crowd had gathered. Smoke puffed out upper windows and I heard a voice of authority.

"Make way, make way. Watch yourself, coming through."

Two firemen in yellow-trimmed black slickers and fire hats hustled an unconscious woman on a gurney through the onlookers.

Everyone tried to get a look at the victim.

Someone near me commented to a friend...

"I pity the asshole who owns that car out there," he said. "Woman dies? He's up on manslaughter...blocking that hydrant, slowing these guys down."

Who? What car?

Then I saw it.

My car.

Sitting in the middle of Sixth Avenue with a wide chain wrapped completely around it.

Jesus.

"Manslaughter!" fired through my head.

And a new thought: the pictures. Associated Press.

First things first.

I looked around.

No one knew I was the owner of the big blue car with the chain around it. The criminal car. The cause-of-death car. The car that would surely be headlines within hours.

What to do.

I bobbed up and down in a pool of curious heads... hmmmmmmm...

The man behind me had on a workshirt that said "Kinney."

Kinney had parking lots all over the city. Including one on the next corner.

I looked at him.

"That's my car out there," I said.

"That your car?"

"Yes."

He smiled.

"Nice."

"Yeah. And, I'm late for work."

"Good luck."

"Are you working at the parking lot today?"

"Supposed to be."

I reached in my pocket.

"Here's my keys and five dollars. If things cool down and they take the chain off my car, would you please drive it into your lot and I'll pick it up when I get off?"

"Man, I can't promise nothin'..."

"That's OK."

"I'll try, but..."

Then he took the keys, the money, and I ran through the fire trucks to the other side of the avenue and the Associated Press.

By the time I left work it was 9 p.m.

Most important, I still had my job.

But, in and out of the day's excitement I'd thought about my car.

Wondered where it was. If the guy got it. If the cops had it and were searching out the registration for the owner who, through his own self-centered parking job, had managed to kill a lady today.

As I quick-walked toward the Kinney lot I was tense.

The chain link fence surrounding it came into view. Through the fence I could make out a few cars.

Bright floodlights lit up the tops of a hundred.

Where's mine. Got closer...walk, look, on tiptoes, heart rate up...

Suddenly, a car top different from all the others. A convertible top...black...it's gotta be me. Proof. Need proof!

I rounded the corner to the lot's entrance.

Inside to the left, the attendant's small shack. Light on.

I stopped, scanned quickly.

THERE IT IS!!!!!!!!!!!!

Yes, sitting peacefully, front facing out, all lined up just like the others was my car.

Oh, god, thank you. What a gift.

How did he do it?

How can I thank him?

I headed for the shack to try.

The flimsy wooden door was one step up.

I pulled it, my mind shuffling the words I would use to express my relief and my impossible gratitude.

My foot clomped across the threshold.

A hanging light bulb lit the face of my brave and fearless hero.

He looked up.

I was about to speak, when suddenly he recognized me.

He stood.

I stopped.

"Dickhead!" he screamed.

"What?"

"Whaaat?" he mimicked.

"I..."

He pushed past me, slammed open the shack door, stepped outside.

Waving his arms. Walking fast.

I followed.

"...so I go out in the middle of the fucking street, risk my goddam life, cops everywhere, jump in that piece of shit, drive off like a sonofabitch for...FIVE FUCKING DOLLARS...and what happens?"

Here he stops walking and raps heavily on the fender of a severely damaged Coupe de Ville.

"No brakes, you sorry asshole...no f-u-c-k-i-n-g bra..."

*   *   *

The next day I drove the car to a Buick dealership and parked it in the last row of used cars alongside a 1958 Ford.

I took off the license plates and could not help noting that the large chrome "breasts" on the front of the car were still shiny and almost blemish-free.

But the car's problems had become "one thing after another," and now that it needed a master-cylinder the time to part ways had come.

The junkyard would have charged $5 to take it away.

I stuffed the license plates into my jacket and got in my brother's car.

We went to a diner, sat at the counter and ordered two burgers, fries, and two Cokes.

Down a few stools two guys were talking.

One said, "Did you hear they shot that guy into space yesterday?"

It wasn't until later that night, lying on my bed in my parents' quiet house, that the insanity of what I'd done the day before began to sink in.

Driving a car with questionable brakes from here to New York seemed almost too much to fathom.

I had come within a rabbit's foot of killing, and being killed.

I wouldn't have been fired if I hadn't made it to work on time.

Why did I take the chance?

I did it because I didn't want to be late to this job I loved, where I felt valued.

This wasn't selling slippers.

Without realizing it, the quality of person I saw and talked with daily at TIME had become my new standard.

TIME writer Calvin Trillin was only 26. Just seven years older than me. When TIME's science writer would go on vacation, Trillin would step in and write the "Science" section. When the writer of "Sports" was gone, Trillin would write sports, same with "Art," "The Nation," "Medicine" and other sections of the magazine. Nights and weekends Trillin would be at the Italian Street Fair in Greenwich Village, the christening of a new ocean liner, or at some obscure, quirky gallery opening.

Trillin was excited by everything life had to offer and, it seemed, was missing nothing.

Though I still had no concrete idea how I'd like to spend my workdays, I was getting hints, and I could see that to be part of the world at anything like a Calvin Trillin level, daily in touch with and working with brilliant people, able to explore any aspect of our culture that moved me, I had to have more to offer both to the world and to myself.

I applied to Columbia University in New York and was accepted.

Twelve months after starting at TIME I put in my notice.

On my last day, they gave me a party that lasted all night.

At 5 a.m. two writers and I went to the Brasserie in the bottom of the Seagram building for breakfast.

At 7 a.m., one of us peeled off at St. Patricks on Fifth Avenue for an early mass, the other walked home, and I took a train back to Connecticut.

It was July, and Columbia didn't start until September.

Suddenly, the next two months of my life were unspoken for.

I was free.

All I could see was the open road and the places I'd never been.

I pictured all the busy diners waiting for me around America… the counters, the jukeboxes, the round stools, the smiling waitresses and the long, plastic menus. I pictured the pies, the cups of coffee, the hamburgers and grilled cheese sandwiches. I pictured the buttes I'd never seen and the cactuses known only from western movies. I pictured listening to country music radio at night in the cab of a semi somewhere in New Mexico and falling asleep in the sun by a river in the middle of nowhere.

CHAPTER 9

Twenty-four hours after my all-night-goodbye to TIME Magazine, Mom dropped me off at the North Street entrance to the Merritt Parkway. I had a gym bag full of necessities and a thumb ready to start a trip across the United States.

Hitchhiking.

In my pocket was $47.

My intent was to go out West somewhere, work and pay for the rest of my adventure.

"Wyoming" had a special ring to it because of all the TV westerns I'd seen, so I headed there to look for a job.

Four sunny days later at 8:30 a.m., I hopped down from the cab of a semi, carried my small brown gym bag into a Wyoming diner and ordered a cup of coffee.

A discarded newspaper sat near me on the counter and I opened it to the "Employment" listings.

Immediately, an ad caught my eye: "High Pay, Easy Work, Travel" with instructions to "See Mr. Beaumont" and an address.

I asked a waitress how to find the place, finished my coffee and walked over to a four-story structure inexplicably called "The Yard."

The building was stone, and tired-looking.

I stepped inside.

No sign of life.

I hollered out for "Mr. Beaumont!"

A pissed-off old voice fired back from way up somewhere, "Get in the elevator, punch four!"

The elevator was the old cage type.

It shook its way upward and jerked to a stop.

I got out.

The fourth floor looked empty.

"Mr. Beaumont?"

"End of the hall!"

I walked down to the end of the hall.

A door was cracked open.

I pushed it and walked in slowly.

Looking for the source of the voice, I saw it to my left…an old man seated at a huge wooden desk and nearly hidden by piles of papers. With a tall bookcase behind him, Mr. Beaumont's squat shape and bald head took up all of a wide rolling office chair.

He twirled an unlit cigar.

"Saw my ad, didja?"

"Yes sir, I did."

"Think you can handle it?"

"Well, I don't know, what is it?"

"It's a goddam gift, a pansy-ass job if there ever was one but I got to hire somebody. Can you drive?"

"Yes sir, sure."

"You lookin' long term, or drifter?"

"I'd like about a month. I'm hitchhiking around the country, need enough money to finish the trip."

"How much is that?"

"About $500."

"Do this job a month you'll make a hell of a lot more than $500 dollars."

"Really. What is the job?

"Well, as you probably deduced by all the books and crap stacked up around here I'm a lawyer, best goddam criminal lawyer in Wyoming. I can get a guy off if he's already confessed and the crime's on film.

"Problem is, once they do get off, some of the bastards can't pay me. So they're mine til they make good, work off the debt. How do they do that? I got a big bad cattle ranch up against the Canadian border. These guys work 14 days straight, come back to town for three days, go back to the ranch for another 14 and so on. Your job is to go get these sorry assholes, bring'em down here, and take another load of 'em back. Are you with me?"

"Yes, sir."

"Up one day, down the next, six days a week. I got one of those half-pint buses, holds about 10 men. You make the big money selling these poor pricks a pack of rubbers, candy, soda, sandwiches, toothpaste, soap, shaving cream, most everything they been dreaming about. Except girls. And you'll make your young ass a fortune."

I took in the office, and his face.

"What'd these guys do to get in trouble?"

"Every goddam thing."

"Killed people?"

"Hell yeah, they killed people. They shot cops, robbed banks, cornholed a sheepdog, any goddam thing. They're just people. Messed up as they might be, they're just people, and people do weird stuff."

Silence.

"What'sa matter?"

"Not sure."

"Not sure what?"

"Not sure I'm the guy for that."

"Think these guys are gonna hurt'cha?"

"That crossed my mind."

"Well, they're not. They're meek as lambs…because they know if they lay a hand on you I'll put their nuts in a blender for life."

The room is quiet.

"Let me think about it overnight."

"Suit yourself. Where you staying?"

"Just got here, don't have a place yet."

"Well, I own the only hotel around here worth drooling on the pillow, you can stay there. Silver Palace. Corner of Ranch and Broadway. One night. When you get there they'll have your room.

"Come talk to me at 9 a.m. tomorrow morning."

"I'll be here. Thank you."

That night was the first time I ever had Ranier Beer. I felt like I was in the real West. And I felt like everyone in that bar looked at me sideways and said, "Pussy."

I finished my beer and left early.

Before I even saw the bed and fell asleep I knew I wasn't going to take that job. He was right. I was afraid. But I had another idea.

Next morning at 9 a.m. I was in the cage punching the button to the fourth floor.

"Morning, Mr. Beaumont."

"Well, are you gonna make some money, or what?"

"No, sir, I'm not."

"I knew that. Be good for you though, you know that, too."

"You may be right." I paused. "May I ask you a question?"

"Shoot."

And then I said something I was ashamed of the minute I let it out.

"Would you consider loaning me $400?

"I'll pay you back when I get a job. I want to buy a small motorcycle and ride it around the country. I'll have a job soon and send you the money right away."

He looked at me as though I had three heads.

He kept staring.

"Son," he said finally, "I have been, and will be, pissed on by invisible dicks...but there's no way I'll be whipped by a scam as obvious as that proposition."

I thought for a minute.

"Invisible dicks..."

"Yes," he said, "you're walking along, doing right, minding your own business...THWAPP!!! something wet lands on your head. You look up...it's all sunshiney...'Hey, this can't be rain!' But it's running through your hair, dripping off your ears. What is it...? Well? It's piss. Where'd it come from?"

He slowly opens his hands.

"Invisible dicks," he said, "happens to everybody."

I smiled.

"I've never heard that before."

He squinted across the desk, a hint of humor in his eyes.

"I'm not surprised," he said.

I could see he was thinking.

"That idea of yours," he said, "it's not so bad. I'm just too old a head, I guess."

I looked across at him.

"I wasn't trying to fool you," I said.

"I know that."

"But, I can see how you took it that way."

He leaned back in his chair.

"What're you gonna do?"

"Get a job."

"Good luck."

I got up from my chair.

He had already tilted forward and become involved with some papers on his desk.

I walked toward the door.

Half of me wondered if I was making a big mistake...if I took that job with him would it be the experience of a lifetime? Would I not get killed after all, or beaten up…or raped, and instead make a lot of money and have a million fantastic stories to tell?

I turned around to say goodbye, but he was off absorbed in his new thoughts.

"When I get where I'm going I'll send you a postcard."

He looked up from the page.

Then he pointed at me with his cigar.

"Thanks, kid," he said, "I'll read it.

Fifty-six days after that morning with Mr. Beaumont, I felt a tap on my shoulder.

I opened my eyes and saw the crewcut Navy lieutenant who had picked me up under a Baltimore bridge a few hours earlier, top down in his baby blue Ford convertible.

"This is your stop, buddy," he said.

I looked out.

We were on the ramp of Exit 3 off I-95.

Greenwich, Connecticut.

My hometown.

"Thank you," I said, "and thank you for the ride."

I reached into the back seat, grabbed my gym bag and stepped from the car.

"Take care of yourself," said the lieutenant as I closed the door.

"You too," I said.

I waved and watched as the car drove away.

A quick shot of wind blew into my face off Long Island Sound.

Suddenly, I had circled the United States by thumb and was back where I started.

I looked around.

Things seemed exactly as I'd left them.

I took a deep breath and began to walk the one remaining mile to my parents' house.

Every step I took was over ground I had walked an incalculable number of times in my life.

But now I had come home from other worlds with many new points of reference.

As I walked, it seemed that every encounter I'd had on that trip had become a movie and that now every one of those movies was fighting for screen-time in my head.

Each story, each moment, queued up for space in my thoughts.

Walking back to my safe and comfortable home, my feet scuffing the sand at the road's edge, I "watched" as each vignette took its turn playing in my memory:

———

At midnight on an interstate outside Chicago a car pulls over and stops a few yards away. I run up, open the back door, peer in and see silhouettes of the driver and another man in the front seat against the dashlights.

"How far you going?" I say.

"Wisconsin."

"Great, thank you!"

I climb in the back and close the door.

With one minute of conversation I learn the two men are in a choral group called The Ray Charles Singers.

Sixty seconds later I am stretched on the back seat, sound asleep.

———

In Montana, under a streetlight, I wait shivering until two cowboys in a Ford Ranchero pickup truck stop and tell me I can ride 30 miles to Missoula in the truck's back bed

It's 30 degrees.

I think for a nanosecond, then take the ride.

For five or 10 miles I freeze and wonder if I can last 30 miles.

They stop the truck and holler back that I can get in the cab.

One gets out and motions me into the center seat.

I look at their faces by the light of the open door: 35 maybe 40 years old, slight beer-buzz in their voices, the smell of cigarettes wafts out of the truck.

I'm not dying to sit between these guys.

But I'm cold.

I do it.

In the middle of nowhere they stop again.

Huh?

They both hop out quickly.

My heart leaps.

I grab my bag and jump down to the road, they casually start taking a leak.

"'S matter, boy," one says, "you shaky?"

The moon is full. The country is empty. I hear unfamiliar sounds.

Get back in?

I look around me.

I don't want to get back in.

But I do.

Only this time I sit by the door.

In the truck, there is just the glow of the dashboard and a silence that scares me.

I have lost track of how far it is to Missoula, my destination.

Rounding each corner, I pray to see lights of civilization.

But there's only more darkness.

One of the men suddenly chuckles and says "John, let's see about this boy…"

The truck swerves into a field at roadspeed, skids sideways, I open my door, jump, tumbling over and over into the grass, get to my feet and run tripping over rock outcroppings and getting up to run again.

The men shout.

A stream of light shoots to my left and I collapse to the ground.

I look back. The truck's spotlight is sweeping across the field.

"We're gonna get your ass you know that, boy, might as well show your face!"

The light waves back and forth.

I hug the ground as close as I can.

Each time the light passes over me I jump up and run farther away.

"You all done but the fun, son!" comes a shout.

What?

Will they bring a light out into the field and find me?

I'm afraid they will.

The sound of my pounding heart will surely give me away.

But they never move.

They yell, they sweep their light, but they do not come for me.

After a while, I hear the truck's engine start.

I peek up above the grass.

I watch the truck back out of the field onto the road and drive away.

I lie flat on my back and look up at the sky.

The sky seems to contain every tiny white-dot star in creation.

I feel the cool air.

My racing heart slows.

I get up and by the light of the moon walk out slowly through the grass, over the rocky spots, to the edge of the road.

I set down my bag and take a deep breath.

In front of me a mountain sits in black silhouette against the starry sky.

I close my eyes, stretch out my arms, work my shoulders back and forth.

For a few minutes I don't move.

Then I pick up my bag and stare down the dark road, hoping for the hint of headlights.

But only headlights coming from the direction opposite the one taken by my friends.

———

Sitting around the dinner table at a ranch where I've just been hired on, I listen to the old ranch hands talk about a boy who had been caught committing "The Infinite Crime Against Nature."

After hearing several tales about this boy and several uses of the phrase "The Infinite Crime Against Nature" I ask what that phrase means.

*After a long moment of silence, the rancher's teenage daughter pipes up,
"It means sex with animals," she says.*

"Oh," I say.

And then, not quite satisfied, I say:

"What happened to the boy?"

Nobody answers.

Around the table people continue eating.

Then, one of the old ranch hands wipes his mouth and looks at me.

"He disappeared," he says.

———

*A four-door Cadillac with a diagonal crack across the wind-
shield pulls up next to me at the edge of an Idaho highway. Inside
the car are seven gypsies. Men and women. All ages. One a baby in
a pink cotton blanket.*

*A handsome, dark-skinned man leans across the front seat and
talks out the open window.*

"Where you heading?"

"Pacific Ocean," I said.

"You drive?"

"Drive? Yes, I drive."

"Drive a car to Pendleton? Meals free."

Pendleton, Oregon? I know that's nowhere near the coast.

*I look at this group all packed together. Serapes, bandanas,
brown bags, soda cans, baby…and the cracked windshield.*

"Yes," I say.

I make the eighth person to get in the car.

I scrunch in the back, half on the lap of an old man.

Next to him is a beautiful gypsy girl about 18.

*We go downtown and on a street corner hook up with two more
men.*

Both have heavy, graying beards.

Neither had a bag or suitcase.

They pile in on top of everyone.

It's hard to breathe and the baby is crying.

Nobody complains.

In a parking lot on the outskirts we rendezvous with three men milling around six late model cars.

The Cadillac's driver gets out.

We gather round him.

"Gonna follow me in line," he says. "I stop, you stop. Nobody passes."

He looks at his watch.

"Noon now, we have dinner 'round six, drive all night."

He looks at me.

"You be last," he says.

He puts me in a brand new two-door Chevy hardtop.

Two-tone, white and copper metallic.

It's a car I'd admired since it came out late the last year.

We make a "wagon train" and set out.

Within five miles we're in desert.

The desert stretches on forever.

We're sticking together. Hour after hour. Forty miles per. The sun is dropping and the light on the hills is palomino-gold, "Green Onions" has played twice already on the radio. My car is fast...but being asked to lope. I see the straight road ahead following up into the hills and pull out into the passing lane where no car is in sight for as far as I can see.

I press the gas pedal to the floor and accelerate past the five other drivers and the gypsy car. I do not look at them. Soon the speedometer is pinned at 115 MPH and I am alone in the glorious wide open Idaho desert sailing on 283 cubic inches of horsepower and 100 decibels of rock 'n roll and a road that 10 minutes later skims off the desert floor and up into a green, wooded forest where I bring the car to a stop by a stream, get out, lean against the fender and wait for the others.

For a long time, I don't see them.

Now there they are.

The gypsy driver gets out of his car and walks to me slowly.

"Why you do that?" he says.

"I couldn't help it," I say.

"Don't do that no more," he says and gets back in the Cadillac.

At dusk we pull into a field of tall grass sprinkled with weathered mobile homes.

The seven cars spread out and stop.

Looking at the trailers I see a narrow rectangular window curtain move.

A young girl's dark eyes peer out. The curtain closes.

The gypsy man steps from his Cadillac.

I roll down my window.

"What are we doing?"

He looks at me.

"Relatives," he says, and goes into a faded yellow mobile home with rust spots on the front door.

Half hour later we're on the road.

Hour after that we drive up to a convenience market.

Two women, one old, one young, go in the store from the Cadillac.

I get out.

"Dinner?" I say.

"Milk," says the young one, "for baby."

At 7 o'clock, we haven't yet stopped for dinner.

Instead, we pull up to a truck-repair garage. A large warehouse-style door is open and the Cadillac drives in.

I park and get out. Our leader approaches a man in overalls and points to his car.

The two walk over and lift the hood.

I get next to them.

"Funny sound," says the gypsy, "hear that?"

"Yeah," says the man in overalls, "but we don't fix cars. Trucks."

"You know what it is?"

The repair man is holding a wrench, he looks at the gypsy.

"Fan belt's flapping," he says.

"Yeah? OK to drive?"

"No, it's not OK. Not if it breaks."

"Can you fix?"

"Yeah, I can fix it, but I don't work on cars."

The Gypsy pulls out a wad of cash.

Two hours later a fan belt has been secured from a neighboring town and we're rolling.

It's 9:30 p.m. at a Big Boy restaurant when we stop for dinner.

I compute that at this rate it will be several frustrating days to Pendleton, Oregon and I tell the Cadillac driver that I will bow out of the troupe and take my chances hitchhiking.

"OK," he says, "but you can eat."

I'm surprised.

We all sit together, he pays for my dinner.

I thank him, pick up my bag, and walk across the street.

Traffic is backed up at the light in front of me.

I wait for the light to change and the traffic to start moving my way.

Maybe someone has room for a rider?

Moments later, on the other side of the highway, I watch as seven cars ease out of the Big Boy parking lot and head toward Pendleton.

The beautiful gypsy girl is driving my car.

On the coastal highway in California a fresh-faced blond surfer picks me up.

He's only a few years older than me but he sells the machinery Brunswick makes to operate 10-pin bowling alleys. It's Friday and he's headed to a mountain lake for a weekend with friends.

"Want to come?" he says.

In three hours we're at a stunning mountain cabin, lakeside.

We lie in the sun, swim, and water-ski at absurd speeds behind sleek, colorful boats powered by Corvette and Cadillac engines.

I am terrified, but exhilarated.

At night it's cool, the cedar trees are tall, we wear sweaters and grill steaks on the deck, we drink beer, talk, and fall asleep on big couches inside by a fire.

In the morning, the beautiful tan mom of one of the boys, wearing a man's white dress shirt over her bikini, cooks us golden, perfectly round, blueberry pancakes.

The small motorbike I bought in L.A. and intended to ride home to Connecticut lies in the grass beside a Riverside, CA highway with a flat ti...

Now I was back in my driveway, walking up our front steps, and through my parents' front door.

I closed it behind me.

Silence.

My eyes went everywhere at once.

In front of me on its long wooden table was the brass lamp where my mom always put our mail or important messages.

I looked around the living room with its white shag carpet, white linen-covered couches, through to the dining room where a copy of a Gauguin painting from his Tahitian period has hung on the wall for years, an image of a native woman in a yellow skirt holding a primitive pot.

The large handmade oval dining table with its rough, charming crack and vase of garden-cut zinnias looked unchanged.

Our eight wooden dining chairs were at odd angles as though we'd all just gotten up from breakfast.

I put down my bag.

"Mom!" I called out.

She ran from the kitchen.

"Oh, Layng!" she said throwing her arms around me.

She thrust me out in front of her and staring with her biggest smile she said, "You look different!"

I laughed.

"I'm different," I said smiling, "but in a good way."

CHAPTER 10

When classes started at Columbia that fall I hit the ground running, and found unexpected benefits.

The Columbia University School of General Studies to which I'd been accepted was a branch designed for people over 20 years old. Ostensibly more mature. Many of my fellow students were older, had families, and had already worked for years. One man in his 60s was an ex-gaucho from Argentina, one a CBS newsman on sabbatical, one an elegant 70-year-old grandmother who came to class in glorious tweeds and so on. A few were kids, most of whom had jobs, and viewpoints formed by a strong dose of urban grit.

As it turned out, the mix added a lot to everyone's education.

My favorite subject was some form of Writing 101. I loved it and got an A-minus, my highwater mark in the land of Ivy League report cards.

Like many of my generation, I was crazy about President John Kennedy. He seemed barely older than we were, like a hugely handsome big brother, and he was president of the United States. Such a change from the great-but-grandfatherly President Eisenhower. I think it made many of us want to be president, too, and he made us believe we could do it. I read every book about him I could lay my hands on, starting with *The Making of The President 1960* and including Kennedy's own Pulitzer Prize-winning *Profiles In Courage* and then *PT 109*, his firsthand account of his harrowing brush with death in World War II.

Left over from my year at TIME was an obsession with President Kennedy's press conferences.

As he was grilled by White House reporters, his charm and humor often drew laughter and diffused what might have been sticky questions.

When challenged about his appointment of his baby-faced 35-year-old brother Bobby to the position of attorney general of the United States, JFK smiled and said, "Well, it'll give him a little experience before he has to go out and practice law."

Few people my age could resist.

All of this fired a great spirit and excitement in young people.

When I decided to go to Washington to research a paper I was writing on Teamsters' president Jimmy Hoffa an amazing thing happened.

My new classmate, the CBS newsman on sabbatical, made me an offer.

"What are you going to do in Washington?" he said.

"Interview people at Teamster headquarters about Hoffa."

"How would you like to see the president's office?"

"Hoffa's?"

"No, President Kennedy's."

I looked at him.

"How?"

"I'm with CBS, I can probably work that out."

A few days later with no fanfare, no paperwork, no apparent screening, I stood with my friend the newsman at the desk of a woman just outside the Oval Office.

He introduced us. The woman must have been the president's famous assistant, Evelyn Lincoln, but I don't remember.

The president himself was not there.

"You can go in," she said.

I looked through the door in front of me into what is surely the most famous room in the world.

"Really?" I thought.

I looked at her, and at my friend.

"Go ahead," she said, smiling.

I stepped onto the oval-shaped carpet and stopped in the silence.

"God…" I thought.

To my left in front of the fireplace was the rocking chair the president sat in so often for pictures, usually talking with other leaders of the world. I walked over to it. There were the expensively upholstered pads on the arms of the wooden rocker, the pads that seemed almost as photographed and famous as the chair itself. I wanted to touch one but I didn't.

I turned around toward President Kennedy's large wooden desk. Slowly I walked over to it and there at one corner was the coconut shell on which he had carved a message after his PT boat was hit by a Japanese destroyer stranding him and his crew in the Solomon Islands. A native had taken the shell with its message to Kennedy's base and all were rescued. The shell was now a paperweight on the president's desk.

I touched it.

The next year, when President Kennedy was killed and lay in state in the Capitol Rotunda, a friend and I drove down to Washington and got in line to walk past the flag-draped casket. It was nighttime when we got there and the line seemed endless. Doubting if we would get to the front before we had to leave, we walked along the line to within fifty feet of the Rotunda's stairs and asked if we could cut in. Someone let us, and in silence, behind the ropes and stanchions, we inched slowly past the mountain of red white and blue covering the coffin of the man who had been our great hope.

I was crying before I even felt the tears coming.

The first day of class junior year I walked up to the third floor of hallowed old Butler Library and into a small room.

Counting the CBS newsman's entrée to JFK's oval office, I was about to meet my second best reason for going to Columbia.

At the end of a wooden conference table sat my new short story professor, smoking like a plane crash. About 60, gray hair cut blunt, no makeup, looking serious and vaguely aggravated, she was the fiction editor of a famous magazine.

"Hi," I said.

"Hi," she said, with a puff and the husk of a trucker.

"I'm Layng Martine," I said. "I'm looking forward to your class."

She nodded her head.

"Welcome," she said, and looked out the window.

I took a seat.

She watched as students drifted in and the nine other seats filled up.

She eyed each new entrant and kept smoking with deep inhales and extended exhales that went on long after everyone was settled.

Finally, she squashed her cigarette butt in her coffee cup and looked right at each face in the room.

"Some people hate smokers," she said, "I hate bullshit.

"I want a paper from each one of you about what you've been doing since you left here in June. Did you piss away your time? Somebody's going to ask me 'How long should this paper be?' So, I'll tell you. It should be as long as a man's leg. Got it? If you horseshit me, I'll quit reading your work."

Some of the kids looked at each other.

I looked at the woman.

I loved her immediately.

She was my favorite teacher (except for Miss Harth, the French teacher who I thought had a crush on me similar to the one I had on her. I cherished that thought until the semester following her teaching my French class when I ran into her in line for coffee somewhere and she didn't remember me).

At Columbia I loved the anonymity offered by a big school in a big city. I loved the people I met on the subway. I loved the proximity to so many bookstores and cafes and music venues and I loved being able to pursue absolutely any whim or idea that crossed my mind, because chances are it was either walking distance or as close as a subway station. Yankee Stadium, The Apollo Theater, poets and folk singers at the Village Vanguard in Greenwich Village. Near school, my favorite hangout was a bar where I went for lunch when I could afford at least five jukebox plays of Ray Charles' "You Are My Sunshine" and their 35-cent hamburgers (served on white bread with lots of ketchup and mayo). I loved the crazed radicals sometimes preaching and passing out incendiary fliers from stepladders at Columbia's Broadway entrance gate.

But despite these flashes of excitement and enrichment, as much as I knew that getting a degree was a good thing to do, and true to my previous run-in with college, my fire for the subjects offered and the required classes gradually cooled. The focus wasn't there. I even had a small business on the side distributing transistor radios and tiny tape recorders I bought downtown from an Indian importer.

Then suddenly, after years of academic sleepwalking at Columbia, my curiosity and ripe emotions led to something that lit me on fire.

It was summer.

I was painting a house.

Standing on a ladder at the second floor level of a large Tudor home I had an epiphany.

My portable radio sat a few feet away from me in a gutter overflowing with rotting leaves.

The song playing out of that radio and most immediately responsible for my awakening was "Abilene" by George Hamilton IV.

Of course, in a way, I was primed.

Primed by fear.

Fear because in six months, with my transferred credits, I would be a senior in college with no idea what I would do afterwards. I had a million passions. The million funneled down to: girls and music, followed closely by wanderlust. How to make a living at any of those was beyond me.

My friends were all enthused about interviews they'd lined up, places they'd been interning over the summer.

American Can Company.

Merrill Lynch.

Burlington Mills.

Just the sound of those words scared me to death.

But, to my friends, those same words sounded exciting.

What would I be excited to do?

As "Abilene" came out of the radio that day, I thought, "That is so good. I wonder if I could write a song?"

Quickly, I said, "Yeah! YES! You can. Do it!"

I have no idea where that came from. I had never in my life thought of writing a song.

But I literally felt my heartbeat jump up.

WOW!!! A DIRECTION!!!!! SOMETHING I WOULD ACTUALLY DIE TO DO!!!!!

I'd been listening to, and loving, songs on the radio for years, singing them in the shower, singing them in my bunk bed at night and as I rode my bike, singing them as I steamed garbage cans at Mount Hermon and on the team bus to games. For years I'd read *Song Hits Magazine* in which the lyrics to the hits of the day were printed. I pored over them and was always amazed at how few words were in these three-minute songs. Of course, I soon learned how hard it was to do that. But when the idea of writing a song first occurred to me, it never crossed my mind that I couldn't write one.

Up on my ladder over the next few days I did.

It was called "Swagger."

Since I didn't play an instrument, I just made up the words and a melody to go with it.

I sang "Swagger" to my mom and my four brothers and sisters who, naturally, told me it was a "Smash!" — which is exactly what I thought it was.

I sang it over and over, in the shower, in my dad's car, late at night walking around our neighborhood, until I could sing it perfectly with all its perceived magic, every time.

I was so excited that sometimes I couldn't sleep, but I had no idea what to do next.

I decided I had to record the song.

But where? How?

In my heart, I knew what I had to do, and I knew where I had to go to do it.

But it scared me to death.

Not because it was dangerous, but because it was just so foreign, so 100% unknown.

"But hey," I said to myself, "do you like the status-quo? Is anything going to change if you just sing your song in the shower and dream about what a big hit it could be? No one will ever hear it."

I knew all that.

But on two separate days, I went to the place I knew might unlock my next step and paced up and down on the sidewalk outside it, but couldn't find the guts to go in.

Until the day I did.

"Your eyes are on FIRE!" the young black man said. He sat on a barstool convulsed in laughter and rapidly slapping his knee with his fingers.

I had just walked into The Turf Bar on Broadway in New York and apparently said something very funny.

Next to him at the bar, his friend chimed in.

"Boy, your ass is GRASS," he said with a giant smile. "You don't even KNOW what you don't know!"

The Turf Bar was a hangout for songwriters, musicians, record people. I knew that because I read all the music magazines.

I'd come here for a reason.

It was 3 o'clock in the afternoon. Twenty minutes ago I'd left my French class uptown at Columbia.

When I stepped into The Turf it was nearly empty. The two black men were alone at the bar.

One had on a long fur coat. The other, a long leather one with a fur collar.

His hair was styled in a pompadour several inches high.

The room was dark.

Both men wore sunglasses.

I walked over.

They saw me coming in the mirror and turned around.

White kid. Corduroys. Button-down shirt.

"Hi," I said, "by any chance are you guys in the music business?"

That's what kicked off the convulsions.

I guess I could have gone to the rest room and let them finish the hysterics.

Finally, they gathered themselves.

"You sharp, boy," one said.

I smiled back at them.

"Yeah," said the other, "we write songs."

I let that sink in.

"I've got a song I want to record," I said. "I wrote it, but I don't play an instrument. I want to hire musicians and a studio somewhere."

A new round of chuckles started.

"That song got music?"

"Yes."

"How it got music, you don't play nothin'?"

They glanced at each other. Much fun.

"I just sing it."

Another look back and forth.

"In the air?" says one.

"Yes."

The knee-slapping started up again, this time preceded by a s-l-o-w high five.

"Do you know what this collar made of?" asked the first young black man, tugging on the collar's edges so I could see.

"No," I said.

"It's ermine, man…ermine. You know how long before you get a ermine collar writing songs?….Sheeeee-it."

When the laughs died down, one of them looked at me and said, "You all right, boy. You all right. Go to Associated, Seventh Avenue. Ask for Milton…he set you up."

With big smiles all around I thanked them, shook hands, walked a few blocks to Associated Recording at 723 Seventh Avenue and took the elevator up to the fifth floor.

I can't remember if Associated had the whole floor, but I can still see the bored and beautiful receptionist chewing gum and reading *Seventeen Magazine*.

"Hi," I said, "I'm Layng Martine. Is Milton here?"

She looked up.

"Milton? Yeah…" she said nodding backwards, "control room."

I stood a second. That's it?

Sure enough, I walked back and found a man stepping out of a room full of knobs and lights and tape reels and a few rolling chairs. Milton. He was about 60, partially bald, wore glasses and a tweed sport jacket.

Hardly my image of an enabler to would-be rockstars.

I explained what I wanted to do, and for about $80, Milton booked my first "demo."

Piano, bass, drums and guitar.

A few days later, in Associated's no-frills all-business recording studio, I sang my song a cappella to the four musicians. They guessed at the chords and wrote them down.

Clearly, these guys had done this at least 5,000 times before.

The piano player ran through a few bars.

"That sound like what you're thinking?" he said.

"That sounds great," I said, amazed that my melody translated in any way to what I was hearing.

The musicians talked among themselves and came up with an arrangement.

"Get on mic," the piano player said, "we'll run one down."

I put on headphones and went over to the microphone.

"One, two…" the drummer counted off.

The next thing I knew they were playing my song.

I heard my vocal with the band playing behind me. Then the engineer added a little echo to my voice.

"What?" I thought, "Is that me?"

Any empty room, any shower stall, any subway station I'd ever sung in suddenly paled.

Heroin? Cocaine? Surely there was no drug as addictive as the one shooting into my ears…

An hour later I held a disc in my hand.

I stared at it.

A label had been glued on.

It said: "SWAGGER," LAYNG MARTINE JR.

For the first time, I didn't wonder what I would do with my life. I went home, lay down on the floor, put two detachable speakers up to my ears and closed my eyes.

Then I played my song for three hours without stopping.

*   *   *

The next day I went to my Columbia classes, but all I could think about was my song and my record. I had it jammed into the pages of my three-ring binder notebook so it couldn't get scratched.

After class, I went into Chock full o'Nuts across from the Columbia gate at 116th St., sat at the counter, ordered coffee, took out my record and looked at it.

"This thing could change my life," I thought.

But how?

What do I do with it?

Since Elvis Presley was my idol, that night I went home, got out my Elvis records and read the business info off to the left on the label, which led me to a company called "Hill & Range Songs".

Hill & Range was the music publisher.

At the time I had no idea what a music publisher was, but I got hold of a New York phone book and found Hill & Range Songs listed at 1619 Broadway, because if that company had anything to do with Elvis, I wanted to go there.

The next afternoon I took the subway from the Columbia campus down to 50th Street and walked two blocks to the address. It was the Brill Building, famous for housing the offices of most of New York's great music publishers and songwriters.

In the shiny brass-walled lobby, I found Hill & Range listed in a brass-framed display case of the building's tenants and walked into the gleaming elevator where a uniformed operator punched my floor.

The lobby of the Hill & Range office was not fancy, but it was a lot more fun than a doctor's office.

Sitting on tables beside the chairs were current and out-of-date copies of *Billboard Magazine* and *Cash Box*, the dual bibles of the music business, along with copies of *Hit Parader* and *Country Song Roundup*, magazines which both contained stories about singing stars and lyrics of the hits.

A girl about my age was the receptionist. I told her I'd written a song I thought would be good for Elvis and that I'd like to play it for somebody.

She disappeared for a moment, then came back and said, "Irwin will see you in a few minutes."

Behind my grateful smile was an invisible double take.

"Can it be this easy?" I thought.

"Irwin" turned out to be Irwin Schuster, on his way to becoming the most famous pop music publisher of his time. Of course, I didn't know that then, and he didn't either, though already he had found and published "Sleepwalk," the instrumental classic by Santo and Johnny.

That day, Irwin didn't like "Swagger" quite as much as I did.

"I like it," he said, "but I'm not sure I hear it as a hit."

You don't?

"It could be a girl's song," I said, not ready to give up.

Irwin thought about that.

"Yeah, I suppose it could," he said.

"Like for The Angels," I said, naming a female group who had just had a big hit called "My Boyfriend's Back." "It could be 'He walks with a swagger' instead of 'I walk…' "

"The Angels are right across the street," Irwin said, "FGG Productions, 1650 Broadway."

That was my cue to get up.

But I didn't want to leave and sat a moment too long.

Irwin stood.

"Come on," he said, "walk with me."

Irwin had on jeans and a white shirt with the cuffs rolled back.

We rode the elevator down, slipped through the ornate lobby and out onto Broadway.

Irwin was a fast walker and I loved striding right beside him.

"I'm taking a promo-pack to a talent agency," he said.

Promo-pack? Talent agency?

"You know," I thought to myself, "this interests me."

The lobby walls of the talent agency were lined with 8X10 pictures of singers and actors the agency represented and in my memory's blur there is no recall of whether any were famous or not.

What I do remember is how much cooler this short walk and this office felt compared to all the other jobs I'd ever heard of…and how much cooler Irwin was than any other "businessman" I'd ever run into.

It was years before I saw Irwin again, but I did follow up on his tip about The Angels' producers being in a building across the street, at FGG Productions.

I quickly learned that "Productions" meant these guys produced records and that record producers are in charge of a singer's recording career, choosing the songs and overseeing the studio recordings.

The "FGG" in FGG Productions stood for Feldman, Goldstein & Gottehrer. Bobby Feldman, Jerry Goldstein, and Richie Gottehrer were about my age but at least 150% more savvy. They'd all grown up in Brooklyn, banded together to write songs and already written and produced one monster hit, "My Boyfriend's Back."

We met when I knocked on their door in a dark hallway of 1650 Broadway, got no answer, walked on in past an empty reception desk and entered their small office.

The three of them were lounging around on the couch and the window sill.

I stopped on the carpet and they looked at me.

"Hi," I said, "I…"

"Hey, man, love those shoes!!!" said Bobby.

Even I had to laugh.

I was wearing saddle shoes, white leather with a brown leather "saddle" in the middle, big at the time among the preppy set, of which I guess I was a member.

I looked down at my shoes, then up at Bobby.

"They're yours," I said.

They laughed.

Richie looked at the disc in my hand.

"You got a song?" he said.

"Yes," I said, "for The Angels."

Jerry took my disc and put "Swagger" on the record player.

The three listened all the way through, tapped their feet, looked at each other back and forth.

When it was over Richie said, "I don't know if I hear it for The Angels, but you got a sound, I love your sound."

Bobby said, "Yeah, man, with those shoes you may be from Pluto or somewhere, but you write good songs. What else you got?"

"That's it."

"That's it?"

"Yes, that's my first song. I'm just starting."

FGG turned out to be my first real "home" in the music business, because in addition to being record producers, they were also music publishers and songwriters themselves.

I became a fixture there and took them all my new songs.

The Columbia campus was a 10-minute subway ride from the FGG office.

The songs were pouring out of me.

My passion had been lit.

I was obsessed. Single-minded.

Early on, that single-minded obsession showed its minuses right alongside its pluses.

Since my mom was a writer, when I was first writing songs, I always asked her opinion on my lyrics. One day I was home and had just finished a new song and walked into her bedroom with the lyrics. I saw her and stopped short. She was lying on the floor.

"Mom, what are you doing?"

She moaned, "I can't move."

"Why not?"

"I don't know," she said, barely able to squeak out the words, "it's my back. Something's wrong."

I stood there for a minute looking at her.

Then I kneeled down beside her, took out a piece of paper, held it where she could read it and said, "Mom…what do you think of this first verse?"

Feldman, Goldstein & Gottehrer were dynamos.

My first recorded song was written with all three of them and called "Lookin' For Boys."

From my standpoint, the idea of girls "Lookin' For Boys" was based strictly on wishful thinking since, to date, no girls actually seemed to be looking for me.

I brought the idea for "Lookin' For Boys" into the FGG office one day in between my Columbia classes and sang them what I had.

"Hey!" Jerry said, "like this, do this!" He sat down at the piano and began to pound out a rhythm and some chord changes and started singing.

Richie and Bobby and I stood behind him pitching in words and melody ideas. The song gelled in a hurry. High fives, dancing, shouts of "monster!" took over the office. That night Richie went home and dreamed up an awesome background part.

"This is a smash for The Angels," Jerry said when we all gathered the next day, "but they're tied up in litigation."

What to do?

They went back to one of their Brooklyn high schools and recruited three adorable girls, named them the The Pin-Ups, taught them them "Lookin' For Boys," recorded the song and put it out on their own label, Stork Records.

The record of "Lookin' For Boys" got to #108 in *Billboard* and earned only pennies, but was a great source of encouragement.

After a few months FGG Productions began giving me a check for $10 a week as an advance against future royalties.

That $10 brought about a most magical change to my life.

Suddenly I was able to get the 40-cent lasagna at the diner across the street...any time I wanted it.

And, after cashing each check at the corner drugstore and paying 25 cents for the privilege of doing so, I still had $9.75 left and would promptly hand back a dime to the clerk and take a jelly donut covered in glorious white powdered sugar...a donut that stands today as World Champion for both flavor and chewy texture.

But, I also got a taste of how a hit record happens.

From start, to finish.

It was 1965 and in the music business, the British Invasion was on. It seemed everyone who was having hits had a British accent. The

Beatles, The Kinks, the Rolling Stones, Dave Clark Five, Freddy and The Dreamers, and on and on.

My three mentors at FGG Productions decided to jump on the wave.

They wrote a song called "I Want Candy," recorded it under the group name The Strangeloves, released it and went on a tour of radio stations pretending to be a trio from Australia...and sporting a wrinkle on the British accent: the *AUSTRALIAN* accent.

The Strangeloves did a blur of radio and TV interviews as these three "outback" characters and the record quickly exploded into a smash.

All of this while I was coming into the office every day in between my college classes.

The Columbia campus is on the edge of Harlem and most every day I passed The Apollo Theater and its marquee boasting of most every act I'd die to see.

Some nights for $1.25 I'd sit in the balcony of The Apollo and watch Little Stevie Wonder (he was 12), Martha and the Vandellas, Marvin Gaye, Bo Diddley, Diana Ross and the Supremes, Wilson Pickett and an endless parade of giant stars work their rhythmic magic.

It was a time in America when black artists were not permitted to play the big "white" venues in many parts of the United States.

A fact of which I was totally unaware at the time.

Wrapped in the same package of energy, charm, skill, excitement as these black singers and songs I loved was a boxer called Cassius Clay, not yet renamed Muhammad Ali.

His confidence, his impish face, folk wisdom and outrageous pronouncements ("I'm so mean I make medicine sick!" "The man who has no imagination has no wings." "I float like a butterfly, sting like a bee.") backed up by his stunning skill and grace, made him irresistible to young people like me.

In one of his last and most famous fights as Cassius Clay, he fought Doug Jones.

I saw that battle in person.

The night of the fight, before heading to Madison Square Garden for the bout, I stopped into former world heavyweight champ Jack Dempsey's restaurant on Broadway for a beer. Like every other night of the week, Jack was there meeting and greeting and I shook his hand. Then, when I got to my seat in the Garden it was next to... elbows touching...Jimmy Brown, the NFL's most famous running back of the day.

"Jesus," I thought, "who would believe this?"

That night, Cassius won a decision over Jones.

For a short time, America had JFK, Cassius Clay and rock 'n roll music.

To a kid my age, those three things together made anything seem possible.

In an uncanny line-up of the fates and as if I needed any more reasons to love New York, a few years after college and during the time Muhammad Ali was suspended from boxing because he'd declared himself a conscientious objector to the Vietnam War, I was standing at the corner of Madison Avenue & 50th Street in Manhattan waiting to meet a friend for lunch. After a few minutes, dressed in suit and tie and carrying a briefcase, Muhammad Ali stopped and took up a spot a few feet away, apparently also waiting for someone. At that time, a sportscaster named Howard Cosell had a daily radio show on which, in his distinctive nasal tones, he regularly asked the sports question of the era, "If Muhammad Ali were to fight Joe Frazier, WHO would emerge the vic-tuh?" Now, desperately wanting to ask Muhammad this question myself, I could soon contain myself no longer. As he stood alone scanning the sidewalk for his friend, I walked up and said, "Muhammad, if you were to fight Joe Frazier, who do you think would win?" My question hit Ali's face like an "ON" switch. Suddenly he affected a mock-shock to his system and looked slowly down at me, puffed up his cheeks and his neck and bugged out his eyes like the friendliest of ogres, then slowly reached for my shirt and necktie and, with them bunched-up in his giant hand, gently lifted me toward his face and in blustery perfection said, "If Joe Frazier so much as DREAM he could beat me…he better wake up and apologize."

His statement made, he eased me down. Suddenly it seemed everyone within 10 blocks flew to Ali like flies to honey.

Wide-eyed, I faded to the back of the crowd, smiling like a Cheshire cat.

The hands and the man that had flattened so many people were also full of fun.

CHAPTER 11

By my junior year at Columbia, I was hooked on writing songs.

And after a long drought, I was also hooked on a girl, named Linda.

Linda's brother Lee had been the beneficiary of my bedroom slipper sale to the Dairy Queen girls years ago on the night we threw the football and he sized me up for his fraternity, and he had become my closest friend during my year at Denison.

Now I was to be the best man at Lee's wedding in LaGrange, Georgia, where his family had moved.

Two days before the ceremony I turned into his driveway and saw his sister Linda through their screen door.

She had dark hair and tan skin. She was wearing an orange empire-style dress, popular at the time, and she stood tall, slim, calm and elegant watching my car come to a stop.

A bomb went off in my heart.

It's the moment I said, "If that girl will have anything to do with me, that's it."

Lady Luck stepped in.

Two weeks after the Georgia wedding, Linda's dad was transferred to New York and she and her family moved to the suburb of Scarsdale, New York, 20 minutes from my parents' home in Connecticut.

We became inseparable.

I'm not sure I ever would have grown up if I hadn't met Linda. Or been a successful person. Or a peaceful and happy one.

When we first dated, I was sloppy and late and completely unable to keep my mind off her, let alone my hands. Like me, she was in college. But she was an art major. And she was a person who actually studied. She knew about painters and architecture and museums and ancient civilizations.

My most cultured aspect was a bent toward jukeboxes, diners, and a few John Steinbeck books.

Linda was peaceful and beautiful and gentle and responsible and wise, and by some miracle she was up for my ideas, each of which seemed totally normal to me but were not on the radar of the general populace. Like driving four hours to Cape Cod with sandwiches, taking a ferry to Martha's Vineyard and riding our bikes to a small wooden bridge where we had…lunch.

That first summer, I was anxious to show Linda all the haunts of my childhood.

By then my parents had moved from our old rural neighborhood to one closer to a railroad station for my dad's daily commute into New York.

I drove Linda the 10 miles back to old our country road, slowed down as we passed the white farm house where Mom and I had lived during the war, past Benny Goodman's house and on to the six acres where Mom and Dad had built our "Modern" house years before.

Those six acres of ours had adjoined the 263 acres of Arthur Hays Sulzberger, owner and publisher of *The New York Times*.

The Sulzbergers had moved to our neighborhood in 1949 in that wave of wealthy New Yorkers who discovered the quiet, natural beauty available just an hour from The City.

For several summers, while mowing, weeding and car-washing on weekends for Benny Goodman and others, along with the rest of a five-man crew I had also mowed the Sulzbergers' lawn and cared for their property.

I drove Linda up the Sulzbergers' three-quarter-mile-long driveway, past the rock cliffs and lawns to the main house and parked behind the equipment garage.

I described to Linda the aristocratic, refined Iphigene Sulzberger, well into her 60s, coming to that garage every Friday with our pay-checks to personally hand them to each one of us.

On the Sulzbergers' land were lakes and hills and massive boulders amid a thick forest.

Mr. Sulzberger built miles of dirt roads through these woods so he could walk and drive through his personal wonderland.

The roads were graded and perfect and extended far across the Connecticut state line into New York.

They were connected to our property and that of our neighbors by a grassy, unused path.

The path ran between two stone walls with barely enough room for a vehicle.

I showed Linda how I would race my car down that path long before I was old enough for a license.

With a portable radio blasting the hits of the day from its perch on the seat beside me, I would thunder between the stone walls and rocket all over Mr. Sulzberger's roads and nearby property at unsafe speeds in my 1948 Prefect, a small English sedan I'd rescued from a field across from our village gas station. The owner was pleased to part with the car for $25. It had flat tires and looked neglected, but it ran.

Through the Sears catalog I bought a paint sprayer. Actually, more of a spitter than a sprayer, stuttering and sputtering out its tiny dots of color. But with it I applied a shiny coat of tan paint to the exterior of the old car, a gaudy aqua blue to the interior door panels, and then painted the inside window frames by hand in a silver metallic gloss.

I named the car "Maxine."

I described to Linda how Maxine and I enjoyed a colorful life until one night a friend threw a bucket of goat feed at my windshield as I sped through his pasture. I lost control, crashed the car and knocked out the front teeth of my 13-year-old neighbor riding in the passenger seat. My parents, and his, agreed that my days as an underage wheelman were over.

At that time, my brothers and sisters and I had played tennis at a graceful old country club just over the New York state line in Westchester County. The country club was on a well-maintained dirt road, and down that road about a 10-minute walk was an old stone chapel.

I loved it.

The chapel was small, with a proper dose of climbing ivy and leaded windows, and designed by someone with a flawless sense of proportion. Maybe it was copied from a chapel in a perfect English village. But maybe it was even prettier than that. The chapel looked calm, settled, peaceful. To be near it was a comfort.

Some days as a teenager I would leave my tennis racquet by the courts, walk over to the chapel, peek in the windows and sit awhile on its front steps.

On one of our first dates I took Linda there.

She loved it, too.

"Let's ride out to the chapel" became something we said often.

We thought of it as our place.

The chapel was far in the country, but some people who commuted to New York City lived out there anyway because the land was so lovely. They lived in hundred-year-old wooden houses surrounded by tall trees and skirted by lawns lined with stone walls left over from when the homesites were meadows. Some of them lived in grand slate-roofed structures overlooking a large natural lake, decorated on summer days by a lone canoe or sailboat or by joyful children jumping off Jacob's Rock.

Commuters rode the train daily to the hurly-burly of Wall Street, Madison Avenue or the fashion world and retreated to these placid woods late in the evening.

Some days Linda and I would ride the 20 miles to the chapel on my motorbike.

Some nights we would drive to it in my dad's old VW bug with the sunroof wound all the way open and the stars clearly visible.

Dappled by sunshine or moonlight, we would sit on the cool stone steps and talk.

The chapel became a metaphor for how we hoped our life together would be.

"This is how I want to live," Linda said one night.

I didn't answer right away.

"Calmly?" I said.

"Yes. Peacefully. With time to be together. Time to hear the crickets."

Once in a while a car would intrude until the rumble of its motor and its tires on the gravel faded off.

"I think we can do it," I said.

"How?"

We leaned into each other, hands between each others' knees against the chill.

"By not wanting a lot of things."

"There's not much I want, except you," she said.

"And a house," I said, smiling and adding one of my own wishes.

"Yes. A little house."

"And a car."

"And a car. But it doesn't have to be fancy."

"No. A car that works."

She smiled.

"And kids."

"Yes. A bunch of kids that look like you," she said.

I kissed her and put my arm around her and we rocked side to side.

"That's a lot," I said.

"I know it. That may be asking too much."

She was quiet.

"Are they the same things you want?" she said.

"Yes, the same. And I'd like to be able to get them doing work I care about."

"Songs?"

"Yes. Songwriting. If I could ever figure out how to make a living at it."

Nobody spoke.

"What about you?" I said.

She looked out onto the chapel's lawn to where the moonlight fell on the pachysandra.

"I guess more than anything I want to take care of you and our family."

"In the big picture," I said.

"Yes," she said, "in the big picture."

"In the small picture?"

"I'd like to design fabrics."

"New York?"

"Yes, I think so."

Our talks went on for hours.

We got to know each other and ourselves, watched over by the chapel's deep walls, its dogwoods and giant sheltering maples.

That's where we set our course, put our dreams into words.

The chapel was our anchor, our reference point, and friend.

And, after the first semester of my senior year, 15 credits from graduation, I quit Columbia because I was in love with Linda, possessed by songwriting, and couldn't imagine how I'd need the degree for anything I would ever do.

My leaving school was a topic never addressed by my parents. Since it was understood that my leaving school ended their financial support, I'm sure they were glad to get me out of the house and off the payroll.

Linda and I were married in the chapel.

The morning opened with rain, but by afternoon the skies had broken into glorious fall sunshine.

Linda's mom threw up on the way to the wedding.

Her sister forgot the marriage license on the ironing board and it had to be delivered to the minister by a state trooper.

But the chapel's guidance has been true.

Even now, we still go back to visit it most summers.

All of our three boys have been there many times.

The road is paved these days.

We park our car and stare at the chapel's strong and solid form.

Linda uses a wheelchair now, I slip it from our car trunk.

We cross the grass and peek in the windows.

Nothing has changed.

Not the simple wooden pews, or the small arched sanctuary where we stood.

We stop on the steps outside.

The ones we sat on so long ago.

The view from the steps seems exactly the same.

Our guardians are still in place: the fieldstone walls, the tall trees, the dogwoods.

And the quiet. Just like we left it.

Together we roll the wheelchair down the brick path where we walked, and where confetti landed on our wedding day.

We can never help smiling.

Sometimes we take pictures.

From the street.

From the lawn.

From the steps.

But we don't need pictures.

Decades after our talks on those steps, Linda and I can see the chapel clearly in our minds.

Wherever we are, wherever we go, all we have to do is close our eyes to be reminded of who we are, and where we came from.

*Fang (right) and me on
the roof of our new house
under construction 1951.*

*"The Original 5"...my
brothers and sisters, John,
Anne, Sue, Fang, and me
1955.*

Linda and me dating, Cape Cod 1964.

Linda's brother, Lee.

Hustling down the aisle in 1965…toward the future.

BELOW

Mom and Dad at our wedding.

Linda treats Benny Goodman to a wedding dance.

Waccabuc Chapel, where we were married.

Ray Stevens and me at BMI airplay awards 1978 when "WAY DOWN" won one.

Our boys, Layngo, Tucker, and Mac with Linda and me at Hershey Medical Center four weeks after Linda's accident.

Kissing my pal at a Watch Hill wedding circa 2000.

Mom at 93.

Fang and me, Quebec City 2016.

Our grandpuppies – Miles, Tennessee, Ryman, and Oz.

Linda and me in "modern times."

CHAPTER 12

Before going any farther I have to tell you that without that "try-just-one-more" habit formed in my door-to-door selling of Cloverine Salve, greeting cards and bedroom slippers, I'm not sure there would have been any revisits to the chapel. That's because the day we got home from our three-day $127 honeymoon to Quebec City my draft notice was waiting for me at my parents' house.

The Vietnam War was on and neither I, nor any one of my friends, could figure out what the United States was doing there. Certainly not why we should give our lives to support that effort.

When Linda and I walked through my mom and dad's front door, thinking we were there to describe to them the great time we'd had on our first days as man and wife, the U.S. Government letter was under one leg of a big brass samovar, an old-fashioned Russian urn used to heat water that Dad had made into a lamp, and where we put each other's mail.

I stopped cold when I saw the envelope.

I stared at it, knowing exactly what it was, then reached for it and tore it open:

"You are hereby ordered to report for Active Duty in the United States Army on…"

I folded it up and looked at Linda and my mom.

"I'm not going," I said.

No one said anything.

"I'm not, "I said. "I'm not dying for nothing."

Finally, Mom spoke in her calm, matter-of-fact tone.

"Honey, military service is the lot of all young men."

"Well," I said, "I'm not going to Vietnam, I can promise you that."

"What do you mean?" she said. "What will you do?"

"Whatever," I said. "Anything. Move to Canada, get in a reserve unit. I have two weeks before I report, if I can get in a reserve unit by that date, I'm okay."

"What?" Mom said.

"Two weeks," I said, "you have two weeks to sign up somewhere else in the military, and if you do, that's your affiliation, you're in the service, and you don't have to report as ordered."

"Who said that?" said Mom.

"Mom, any guy knows that. People are dying."

Linda and I had no mortgage, no kids, no tie-downs to keep us nailed in any one place.

"We can live anywhere," I said.

Even though joining a reserve unit meant a six-year commitment to the service, except for six months of active-duty the commitment was only for weekend meetings once a month.

We went home that night and I made a plan. I would start with the least populous states — Wyoming, Montana, the Dakotas — and call every reserve unit in every one of them until I find one with an opening. Surely the reserve units in those empty places could not all be full.

I sat with my dial-phone and called AT&T "Information" over and over and over until I'd gotten the phone numbers and called every single reserve unit in those four desolate states.

My music publisher volunteered to pick up the tab for the outrageous long-distance phone bill I was building.

Not one reserve unit offered even a glimmer of hope.

"Sorry, we're wait-listing now…"

"Been full for two years."

One sergeant laughed when I asked if they had an opening, "Is this a prank call?" he said.

Days ticked by.

I kept calling.

When I crossed out the last phone number on the list I stopped to re-think.

Since the less-peopled places had seemed such obvious possibilities but had yielded zero results I decided to make some random calls and see if I could pick up any information.

A lieutenant in Vermont said, "If you can wait a month or two I might have something."

I explained I had 6 days until I had to report.

"Sorry, son, can't help you there."

"Lieutenant," I said, "got any thoughts? Any idea who might have a spot…anywhere in the country?"

He was a thoughtful guy and he paused a second.

"Hell, our demand's about as light as anyone I talk to, most everybody else is over the top on waitlist."

I hung up the phone.

I thought about all the reserve units in America.

"Somewhere," I said, "somewhere in the United States there is an opening at a reserve unit. It's impossible that every single one of them is full. How can I tune-up my search?"

That night Linda said "What are you going to do?"

I said, "I'm going to keep calling and I'm going to find a reserve unit with an opening."

The next morning…an idea.

Every state has a defense or military affairs office. I learned that when I was getting the phone numbers.

A thought: "Maybe there's a master list of openings throughout each state?"

I picked up the phone and dialed the defense department in Connecticut. No luck. Then I called a state nearby.

The guy who picked up the phone was a talker. And a listener.

"Sir," I said, "my name is Layng Martine, I'm not trying to duck my duty to the country," I said, "but I was married 11 days ago and got my draft notice to report next Thursday for active duty. I would like to join a reserve unit and wonder if you know of one anywhere in the state that might have one opening?"

"Ahhhh," he said, "that's a problem. Ya got any connections?"

"Like what?"

"Like do ya know anybody that's got a name, power, a little juice?"

I thought of my grandfather and the clout he might've had.

"Jesus," I said, "anybody I might know in that category is dead."

He gave a quick snort-laugh, "That ain't gonna help," he said.

Suddenly, I remembered my grandfather's brother, a guy I'd never met. In our family, he was only mentioned a couple of times in passing, no explanation.

But, this brother was a judge. And, as it turned out, a famous one.

"Wait," I said, "my uncle is a judge."

Pause.

"You just thought of that?"

"Yes…"

"Judge who?"

"Judge O'Connor."

"So…you…are…Judge…O'…Connor's…nephew?"

"Yes."

"Son," he said, "that's a good ticket. Hold the phone…"

A click, and silence.

I held the phone, and my breath, for what seemed like 20 minutes. I wondered if he was ever coming back.

Another click, sudden room-noise and the man's voice, "All right, Judge O'Connor's nephew, give me your full name…"

What? My heart jumped.

"James Layng Martine, Jr.," I said.

"What the hell kinda name is that?"

I laughed.

"A strange one," I said.

"Yeah, you got that right. Okay, here's what you do"

He gave me the address of a National Guard armory.

"Eight a.m. Monday morning. Be there. Ask for Lieutenant McGinniss."

Another long pause.

A fleeting thought that if this didn't work out on Monday I only had three days left before my report-date.

That thought was quickly dismissed.

"Thank you," I said, "it's impossible to thank you."

"Yeah, well, you're a newlywed. Good luck," he said, "and a tip: don't ever get divorced. I been there."

I smiled.

"That's a deal."

Monday morning I got up at 5 a.m. for the 45-minute drive to the armory and got there before 7. I parked my car and walked across the street to a diner for a cup of coffee.

At 8:00 I walked up the granite steps of the armory, pulled open the huge wooden door and went inside.

Not a sound.

Not a person in sight.

I stepped out of the entry hall and into a cavernous room. Huge olive-drab Army troop trucks were packed against the far wall and a vast wooden floor between us lay empty.

I looked around. Nobody.

Above the floor I noticed a mezzanine and the tops of doorways that looked as though they might be offices.

I found a stairway, went up to a hallway and walked along it peeking into the open doors. No people.

At the corner I stopped.

In the corner office behind a large wooden desk with an American flag to his right sat a man in full dress uniform. On his desktop of stacked papers stood a large brass name plate.

"Lieutenant John McGinniss."

I knocked.

"Lieutenant McGinniss," I said, "I'm Layng Martine, told to report to you this morning."

He looked up.

"Yeah, Martine, sit down."

He began flipping through folders.

"I got no idea why I'm doing this," he said, "I got like 500 guys on my waiting list and Defense calls me and says I gotta get you in here because you're Judge O'Connor's nephew. I musta been in a good mood."

I felt my heartbeat jump a little.

"Thank you," I said.

"All right," he said, "info. Full name and address."

I spelled my name, but when I got to my address and it was out of state he stopped and looked up sharply.

"What? You can't have a Connecticut address and be in this unit. Ya gotta live here for Christ's sake!"

Now my heartbeat shot up and I felt my face get hot.

I flipped through my thoughts for what to say.

"I don't have a local address," I said.

"You don't have one?" he said, vaguely annoyed. Then he looked around his desk and found a phone book.

He threw it to me.

"Pick one," he said.

Oh my god, I thought, this is like the movies. I can't do this.

"I'll get one," I said, "I'll be back in an hour."

Lieutenant McGinniss shrugged his shoulders and opened his hands.

"Suit yourself," he said.

At a public phone outside I found a phone book and the listing for "Rooming Houses."

I called three before I found one close by.

For $9 a week, payable in advance, I rented a room and returned to Lieutenant McGinniss with an address.

We completed the forms and he sent me down three blocks for a physical.

The doctor's office was in the basement of a nondescript residence. The doctor looked at me, laid the stethoscope front and back, and pronounced me fit for battle.

Back at Lieutenant McGinniss's desk with my medical papers stamped he said, "All right, we're getting somewhere now." He handed me a booklet and printed piece of paper.

"This here booklet is a test," he said. "Go in that room and take it. The second sheet there is for your answers. Take you about 30 minutes, and I'll swear you in."

Holy shit, it's really going to happen.

I went into a small dark room off Lieutenant McGinniss's office, searched for a light switch, sat down and began the test.

Half-hour later I walked out and handed Lieutenant McGinniss my completed answer sheet. He laid a correct-o-sheet over it and, through punched-out holes, counted the spots darkened by my pencil. Those darkened spots were my right answers.

When he finished counting and looked up, his face was tight and flushed.

"You nervous?" he said.

"Yes," I said, "a little bit."

"Because you flunked the test."

"You're kidding."

"I'm not kidding."

What? Whaaat?

"Jesus..."

We looked at each other for 10 terrifying seconds.

I wanted to scream, "No!"

The Lieutenant looked out the window. His left hand messed with the pencils on his desk.

I sat staring at him and imagined Vietnam, bullets, trying to kill people, dying.

How did I blow this? It was a GIFT!

Suddenly he looked back at me.

"You been to college?"

"Yes," I said.

"Then you got enough brains to pass this test. Go in there and take another crack at it."

Did...he...really...just...say that?

I stood up and went back to the room.

Thirty-five minutes later I came out and handed the test sheet to Lieutenant McGinniss.

He laid a correct-o-sheet over my answers and counted the dark spots with his pen.

His count seemed to take an hour.

Then he finished and looked up.

He pushed back in his chair.

"You passed," he said, sick of the subject.

I wanted to hug him, or thank him, or cry, or lie down for two weeks and try to feel normal again.

But I stood up next to the flag, raised my right hand, and Lieutenant McGinniss swore me in.

Then he shook my hand.

"Congratulations, Martine, you're now in the United States Army. First meeting is next Saturday 8am."

"Thank you, Sir, I will see you then."

One minute later I was in our ancient red Volkswagen speeding for home.

The backed-up traffic on the interstate, normally cause for swearing and frustration, didn't faze me. Nor did the long lines at the toll booths. A lengthy detour off the highway wound around residential streets for 45 minutes before leading back to the four-lane.

I didn't bat an eyelash.

I was not going in the Army in three days like that letter said I was and no amount of aggravation could pop my bubble.

Back in Connecticut, I raced in our driveway and ran upstairs. Linda was in the kitchen.

I stopped short in the doorway.

"YOU," I said, "are looking at a soldier!"

Her eyes got wide and she dropped her dishrag...

"They took you?"

"Swore me in!"

"That's incredible!"

"It is incredible..."

"Vietnam?"

"Unlikely."

She wrapped her arms around me and I wrapped mine around her.

It was a year and a half before I went off for six months to be trained as an infantryman. And Fort Dix, New Jersey was the closest I ever got to Southeast Asia.

*   *   *

Between hitchhiking across the country, public school and my many jobs, I'd been around all kinds of people who were very different from me. But, my first reserve meeting was still culture shock.

About 20 of us were new inductees, did not yet even have uniforms.

After we'd been sitting in a row of bleachers for two hours, a sergeant about 5'6" came over wearing full combat gear, including his steel helmet. A small metal replica of a rifle was pinned to the front of his fatigue shirt. From the pin, awards of some kind dangled and swung back and forth when he walked or moved.

He looked like a miniature soldier as he stopped in front of us, stared, and put on his toughest face.

"Peons!" he shouted, "Dust particles! Stand up, group around me!"

Everybody shuffled into a circle, our new leader at the center.

He stood there, M-16 on his shoulder, so short that anyone not in the first circle couldn't see him.

"All right, you assholes," he hollered, "listen up. I have information for you. You belong to me now, all right? YOU…are mine. In case you ain't figured it out, we are the United States Infantry. We shoot people, and we get shot at. My job is to keep you safe, win wars. As you might read in the papers, reserve units do get called up, do get activated, do go to the war zone, and if we go to Nam, here's how it is: I say swim a river, you swim a river. I say dig a hole, you dig a hole. I say climb a rubber tree, take a hill, crawl through mud jungle or run toward gunfire, you…"

Just then, a big Italian kid behind me taps me on the shoulder and whispers in my ear, "We go to Nam? Foist thing I do? Shoot that fuck."

CHAPTER 13

The tiny sergeant was an indelible character. But our first year of marriage gave us two other unforgettable human beings who were a bit closer to our hearts.

As the crow flies, our first home as newlyweds was 12 minutes from the steps of the chapel where we were married, in Jim and Margery Erickson's large stone house in the back country of Greenwich.

Linda and I lived on the Erickson's third floor.

Most nights, Mrs. Erickson ate dinner alone by candlelight, dressed as though giving a lovely party.

She sat at the head of her long antique dining table. On one side of her was a floor-to-ceiling John Singer Sargent painting and on the other were two small birds tweeting and rustling softly in their cage.

The Ericksons' five children were grown and gone, though a beautiful daughter at college nearby would occasionally stop by on weekends.

Some nights from her dinner table Mrs. Erickson would hear Linda and me come in through her kitchen door, heading for the back stairs to our rooms and call out, "Linda, Layng, would you like to join me?"

On these nights, she might have cooked escargots or lamb chops enough for all three of us. There, at her gleaming table with its fresh flowers in the center and the John Singer Sargent portrait on the wall seeming real enough to be another guest, we talked about love, our hopes, and our dreams. She told us about the years she and her husband had spent on a lonely white-bleached island in the Caribbean where Mr. Erickson had gone to seek his fortune in the mining of salt.

We met Mrs. Erickson because of a classified ad she ran in the Greenwich newspaper.

The ad said: "LIVE FREE IN EXCHANGE FOR WORK" and a phone number.

It was late fall and chilly the night we drove out to her house.

The driveway was lined with dogwood trees. In our headlights the road curved past a pond and eventually back to the three-story stone house where we parked on a graveled circle next to an older model Mercedes.

We walked up two wide flagstone steps, stopped beneath a lighted white portico, and rang the bell.

We heard 10 seconds of footsteps before Mrs. Erickson opened the door. She was tall and elegant. Her clothing seemed from a bygone time, as did her gentle, welcoming demeanor and accent, which was nearly British in its lilt. She took our coats and showed us into a wood-paneled library with low lights, cozy couches, chairs, and a roaring fire.

"Well," she said, settling into the deep pillows, "I'm pleased to meet you both and I'm so glad you answered my advertisement."

"We were thrilled to see it," I said. "We're going to be married in a few weeks and the prospect of earning our rent through work is a wonderful thought."

Mrs. Erickson smiled.

"The work will not be anything strenuous. Layng, I'd like you to plow the drive when it snows…we have a Gravely tractor in the garage. And Linda, when I'm away I'd like you to water the plants and feed the birds. You see my husband, Jim, is an adventurous man. He travels a great deal for business and sometimes…though rarely…I go along with him. He goes mainly to China and the Far East. When he does, I'm by myself."

"And," I said, "as far as the other jobs…"

She looked at us matter-of-factly.

"I think that will be enough."

It was the start of a grand friendship.

The first time we saw Mrs. Erickson's husband, Jim, he was five feet from us, outside our window.

Our third floor window.

Jim was standing in the limbs of a huge pine tree where he had climbed to prune branches.

"Hello!" he called, smiling broadly.

"Hello!" we called back.

"I'm not supposed to be up there," he told us later. "The doctor says my heart won't take it. But I've done this all my life and have no plans to stop now."

Mr. Erickson was tall and handsome, with thinning hair and a regal confidence that was softened beautifully by his crinkly smile and gentle way. His bearing and twinkling eyes assured the observer that if ever there were a problem, chances are it would be no match for him.

When Mr. Erickson was home we would sometimes see him with Mrs. Erickson having lunch together on the sunny stone terrace.

Sometimes in winter they would ask us down for a drink by the fire.

He would sit beside her on the couch, arm across her shoulder.

And he would wait on her hand and foot.

Often, as we passed through their kitchen on our way to the back stairs, the Ericksons would be cooking dinner together, chatting, crystal wine glasses in hand.

Sometimes their laughter would echo up to our rooms.

For two years, Linda and I lived in the Ericksons' glorious house.

The sound of birds singing and the air of the changing seasons blew in through our open windows and across our pillows and our faces morning and night.

We painted our bedroom yellow because a friend said that was the happiest color to wake up to.

The Ericksons installed a wood stove for us which added heat (and charm) and they didn't mind when Linda painted our kitchen walls with 10-inch-wide black and white stripes, or when we gave small dinner parties...sometimes inviting the Ericksons...or that all our guests had to pass through the Ericksons' kitchen to reach the back stairs.

The intruders were greeted with hearty Ericksonian huzzahs as they slipped through to our back stairway.

And in warm weather the Erickson's didn't mind when we stepped out one of our windows onto the roof of their large sunroom where we grilled hamburgers.

Each morning Linda and I took the train to New York and came home at night to our haven in the treetops.

But active-duty in the Army reserves finally beckoned, and after a year or so Linda was living there alone.

I was at Fort Dix, New Jersey being trained as an infantryman.

On my first weekend of home-leave, I was in my dress uniform Sunday afternoon heading out to meet my ride back to the base. Linda and I were going down the rear stairs when Mrs. Erickson intercepted us on the second floor. Her normally elegant hair was askew. She was in her gardening clothes and had smudges of dirt on her cheek and white shirt.

She was calm, but spoke firmly.

"Jim is in the garden," she said, "and I don't believe he's living. Linda, would you please call an ambulance. Layng would you please go to Jim."

When I reached the garden I saw Mr. Erickson lying on his back, his tan lean body dressed only in khaki shorts and sandals.

His face was already blue.

I threw my Army hat to the ground and kneeled down over him.

Five days ago I had learned mouth-to-mouth resuscitation in basic training.

I reached into Mr. Erickson's mouth and held his tongue with my left hand. I pressed my mouth to his and forced my breath into his lungs. With my right I pushed down on his chest, let up, pushed down. No response at all. I kept at it until I felt a hand on my shoulder and heard a voice say, "All right, soldier, I'll take it from here."

I looked up at an EMT in a green uniform.

I stood.

Linda was a few feet from me.

Mrs. Erickson was coming toward us across the grass. She had already changed into a long formal dress, white gloves and a large formal hat which was brown with a white flower attached to the hatband.

She stopped a few feet from her husband and watched as two EMTs laid a sheet over him.

Gently the two men moved Mr. Erickson onto a stretcher and carried him through the open back door and into the ambulance.

Mrs. Erickson looked at Linda and me as she moved forward.

"I'll ride with Jim," she said.

Mrs. Erickson lifted her long skirt, walked up the ambulance ramp, ducked her hat, stepped inside, sat down on a bench beside Mr. Erickson's covered body, folded her white-gloved hands, and the EMT shut the door.

Along with his last will and testament, Mr. Erickson had left instructions for his funeral.

I was at Fort Dix that day, but Linda went.

A Dixieland Band played on the back terrace and a festive lunch was served in the sunshine on white tablecloths.

A few months later, Mrs. Erickson put her house up for sale, we moved out, and we lost track of each other.

Linda and I bought a small house of our own, had a baby and got caught up in being parents and earning a living.

A few times, we tried to find her, but she had left Greenwich. It was pre-internet and we never connected.

But the kindness of the Ericksons, their sweetness with each other, and our happy years in that refined and loving home were things we referred to often, both in our thoughts and in the way we went about our life together.

Mrs. Erickson and I did speak one last time.

It was was about eight years later.

She must have been 60 or so.

By then, we had moved to Nashville and I was a songwriter.

She got our number from my parents who still lived in Greenwich and she called because she had written a song.

She sent it to me and I read it and gave her my thoughts, which is what she wanted.

"Where are you living now?" I asked.

"I've remarried and my new husband and I live in Watertown, New York."

I remember how my heart leapt and how I smiled there in our small kitchen when I heard that.

"Mrs. Erickson, that makes me so happy," I said.

There was a long pause.

"You're good to say that, Layng" she said.

"You and Mr. Erickson were such an example to Linda and me."

"Yes, he…"

She gathered her thoughts.

When she spoke again, it was with the same strong voice I'd heard so often in the beautiful dining room of her beautiful house.

"My new husband is not a kind man like Jim," she said.

For nearly 40 years that was the end of the story.

But then, thanks to the internet, I found the Erickson's beautiful daughter.

The daughter who was in college and who sometimes dropped by her parents' home on weekends.

She's in her 60s now. I haven't seen her. But somehow I believe she's still beautiful.

When I said my name into the phone, she said, "Yes, Layng, I remember you...it was Linda who told me my father had died."

"I didn't know that."

"Yes, I had driven home unexpectedly that Sunday from college..."

"I remember that day so clearly, being in the garden with your Dad..." I said.

A moment of silence.

"Yes," she said, "I remember it so clearly, too."

She was quiet again before speaking.

"Did you know my father was losing everything, on the verge of bankruptcy, that day when his heart gave out?"

. This time, it was me who paused a long time.

I thought of the Ericksons' house.

I thought of Mr. Erickson's face. His smile. His twinkling eyes. The magnificent way he held himself.

I thought of our first glimpse of him up in the pine tree.

I thought of him on the couch with his arm around Mrs. Erickson, and of his fit body lying so still in the garden.

"No," I said, "I didn't know that."

CHAPTER 14

During the two years we lived in the Ericksons' house, much changed.

In the beginning, Linda was a fabric designer in New York and it wasn't long before her designs of sheets, bedspreads, draperies, rugs and carpets were in Bloomingdale's, Macy's, Greenwich Village boutiques and on the floors of the Plaza Hotel and the New York Hilton.

On our first Christmas, Linda gave me my first guitar. I learned the rudimentary chords that made up most all the songs I loved, like "Johnny B. Goode," "Whole Lotta Shakin'," "Hound Dog."

I met a wonderful new music publisher and a few blocks away from Linda's Lexington Avenue design studio I was now writing songs for a division of CBS.

And, even though a few days a month I planted trees and shrubbery for a local nursery to earn extra money, every other day I walked into my cork-lined cubicle at CBS, turned on a dim light for atmosphere, and wrote songs.

An older songwriter, balding and pipe-smoking, was often at the CBS office.

His name was Lou.

Lou was there to work with his co-writers.

"Hey," he said one day, "you should write with me."

I didn't want to write with anyone.

"Well," I said, "that's flattering, Lou, thank you…"

"Hell yeah, it's flattering…"

His blustery words, always delivered with a smile, had a certain charm but I paid little attention because I was having a good time writing alone.

Then a few days would pass.

There he was again.

"Layng, when are you going to write with me?"

"I don't know, Lou," I said, "I'm kind of a loner."

"Oh, yeah? How ya doin' out there by yourself? Got a lot of hits coming out?"

I smiled. Of course I had no hits coming out.

He looked up from his seat on the sofa.

"I write hits," he said.

And he had. Two of Lou's hits I particularly loved, "Round and Round" by Perry Como and "The Treasure of Love" by Clyde McPhatter.

Next thing I knew I was headed to Lou's $77-a-month rent-controlled apartment for what turned out to be extremely helpful songwriting lessons.

Of course, Lou called what we were doing "co-writing."

And it was.

But during our writing sessions I learned so much. I often felt those get-togethers were more like songwriting classes.

Lou and I would complete a song and I would go home and take it apart to see exactly how it was constructed, how he built up the verse into the chorus, what chords he used (all simple ones that I already knew), how the story got told clearly and quickly.

Lou and I wrote six or seven songs over a few years and I think five of them were recorded, though no hits.

The activity around the CBS office was exciting and I felt at the center of something special.

My cork-walled office adjoined an identical office occupied by a songwriter named Chip Taylor.

One day our publisher, David Rosner, knocked on my door.

"Layng, I just got a recording from England of one of Chip's songs, I'm going to play the record for Chip in my office, do you want to come?"

Chip and I stood in front of David's desk as David put the record on.

It was "Wild Thing" by The Troggs, soon to be the number one record in the world.

As the record played, the sound and excitement leaped off the vinyl from the first guitar downstroke. I looked at Chip.

"Holy cow!" was an understatement.

Hearing that original version of "Wild Thing" at the same moment as Chip, the writer, is unforgettable, especially since the song is now one of the most ubiquitous and iconic of all rock songs.

Despite the great excitement that often resonated in the halls of CBS' music publishing offices, most of that buzz was for other peoples' songs.

Nine months after our wedding day, CBS decided that my small advance had me too far in the red and I was let go.

*   *   *

When that happened, I had a sudden longing for stability.

I tried to bury my need to write songs and focus on staying afloat.

Linda helped me make a "book" of ads that I could take to an employment agency to see if I could get a job writing advertising. I wrote the words in the book; she drew the pictures.

I got a good job with a famous agency on Madison Avenue.

I was assigned to write ads for the Maidenform bra account.

Determined to succeed, I pounded out Maidenform ideas and slogans on my typewriter like a fiend.

Proof of just how unsuited I was for this assignment and just how forgettable were all my ideas and slogans is the fact that I can remember…none of them.

I nearly lost the job immediately.

It was quickly clear that I had no feel for what it was like to wear, or need, a bra.

The words I wrote drew baffled stares from my boss, a beautiful woman named Martha.

My job was saved by another woman who was later reported to have had a few pops that day at lunch.

At a meeting called to discuss my firing, she bucked the others and said, "The kid's on bras! How would you like it if you got a job writing advertising and the first day you showed up they put you on jockstraps?"

The women switched me to cookies where I was quite at home.

Over the next four years, I wrote print ads and TV commercials for cigarettes, window cleaner, laundry detergent, bread, tea and women's laxatives, as well as the bras and cookies.

At first it was a relief to have a steady paycheck.

Since we were still living free at the Erickson's, we had spending money.

On regular weekend drives to Maine, Vermont and anywhere else that moved us, Linda and I rarely passed up a chance for clam rolls, ice cream, blueberry pancakes or other roadside delicacies. For a cheap taste of France, we thought nothing of an eight-hour sprint to Quebec City late Friday and being back at work on Monday.

A year or so into my advertising job, the head of the agency decided I was a valuable asset to the company. So when I had to slip off for my six months of infantry training at Fort Dix, he sent Linda my full bi-weekly paycheck and I sent him my meager monthly check from the Army.

During the Army physical I was the only guy who didn't want to flunk, because Linda and I were planning to bank every nickel of my advertising paycheck while I was away, which we did. With no rent to pay, by the time I completed my training we had saved up a small bundle and went to Europe on our first big vacation.

Once out of the Army and back on Madison Avenue, and in an ongoing effort to shake the need to write songs and plant both feet in an advertising career, I read classic books on the subject of writing print ads and TV commercials.

From Rosser Reeves I learned the concept of a "Unique Selling Proposition." I studied David Ogilvy's insights on what makes a great adman. In some ways I saw myself in these books. In other ways not. David Ogilvy described a young guy who worked on the Esso account (now Exxon). He said this devoted advertising writer would spend his weekdays working at the ad agency, and then on weekends he'd climb into overalls and work at a service station squeegeeing car windows, changing oil, putting air in tires and pumping gas...feeling Esso's business at ground level.

Ogilvy said that if you were the kind of guy who went home and spent weekends with your family he might like you better as a person, but the other guy would do better in business.

I suspected I was the guy who would opt for home.

Gradually, doubts crept in about the value of my work, about how I was spending my days.

Does the world really need another detergent, another cigarette?

Is this what I wanted to be doing?

And then a day came along to answer my questions.

One of our products was a famous window cleaner.

Windex was the leading brand and our main competition. At the time, Windex advertising leaned heavily on the fact that it contained ammonia.

In our meetings, I and my fellow ad writers often pleaded with our client to give the window cleaner we advertised an ingredient that would offer a competitive edge.

After months of begging, a big meeting was called to announce a breakthrough addition to our product.

At the appointed hour, we all gathered around a conference table to hear the news.

After a moment of settling in, the account executive for our window cleaner stood up.

"All right," he said, "you guys have been whining for something to talk about, something to differentiate us from the competition… well, now you've got it. By 9 a.m. Thursday I want 10 new commercials using the tag line, 'New with MORE AMMONIA'."

Silence.

The account executive seemed stunned.

"So…is that all I get? Silence?"

A momentary pause.

A writer raised his hand.

"John," he said, "do we have more ammonia than Windex?"

John's face got flush.

He tilted his head as though addressing a misbehaving child.

"No, Ralph, we do not have more ammonia than Windex."

Ralph stared back.

"So…more ammonia than what?"

John looked right at him.

"Ralph," he said, "we have more ammonia than we had last week."

The room broke out laughing.

I went home that night, flopped down on our bed and buried my head in a pillow.

"I feel like I'm wasting my life," I said to Linda.

And, far from letting up, my craving to write songs had only accelerated.

One day I'd walked into a Broadway record store and, flipping through the newest crop of album releases, I found one with the same title as one of my songs, "Let The World Go By."

In fact, it was my song.

It turned out to have been submitted to a famous folk singer (Glenn Yarbrough) by CBS, my old publisher, then recorded without either of us knowing it.

The feeling I got from finding that album, getting that news, was so far superior to any satisfaction I felt from the advertising I'd been writing that there simply was no comparison.

And, though the earnings from the album were miniscule, there was no doubt that this was the rush I was after.

I began staying in New York late after work and writing songs with an assortment of people.

I found I was a pretty good singer.

Though I did not want to be a stage performer I loved singing in the studio, making records, and was even signed to a few labels, with singles released, but none clicked.

Several other recordings of my songs developed, including one by Bo Diddley, and while none of these were big moneymakers either, songwriting owned my heart.

The problem was, I had no idea how to make money at it.

That problem was compounded by the fact that we had bought a house, a duplex for which the rental side nearly paid our mortgage, but we also had a new baby and Linda had decided to stop working and be a stay-at-home mom.

We needed regular income.

So, five years after we were married, as a new dad trying to make a life doing what I loved and also have a family and the freedom to be part of it, I made a costly wrong turn.

At that time, something called "franchising" was a big thing.

Someone with little or no experience running a business could buy a copy of a business that was already successful, open it up in the exact image of the successful ones, and theoretically replicate their success.

In a perfect world, the "Franchisor" or parent company, the entity that sold you your business, would train you, line up your suppliers and "be there for you, baby" all along the way until you were up 'n' running and could thrive on your own.

In my desperate state, I landed on a franchise called "CHEEKY'S Fish Tacos."

At that time you could get into an CHEEKY'S franchise for peanuts, so I quit my perfectly good job in the advertising business and bought a CHEEKY'S Fish Tacos franchise.

And soon added another.

After all, in my read of the CHEEKY'S sales mantra, the shops would "run themselves."

A business that "ran itself" was just what I needed.

Feeling lost and trapped at the time, I was flailing for some way to pay the bills while I wrote songs.

My theory was that I would visit my new fish tacos shop every Friday to pick up the money.

The rest of the time it would be run by my devoted and dependable staff who would, of course, know how to cook and serve the fish while charming the hordes of happy customers.

That was my plan.

What happened, naturally, was a lesson. The lesson had something to do with staying away from things you don't know anything about and have no interest in.

Occasionally, I found time to cry about the mess I'd made for myself. But only when I wasn't under siege.

Mostly?

I was under siege.

I had customers who plucked their own turds out of the toilet and threw them at our restroom walls, managers who skipped town with a weekend's receipts, an entire car that came through the restaurant's wall and settled in our dining area.

All this was routine stuff for an experienced restaurant man, but disruptive for a wanna-be songwriter.

And then there were enduring events that let me know for sure that I was in the wrong business.

One night at the store, I answered the phone and heard the voice of the man who lived behind the restaurant.

"Mistuh Mahteen?"

"Yes."

"It's Mistuh Wurmtusch."

As if he had to tell me.

Mr. Wurmtusch had been calling several nights a week for months.

Several times he had popped in during dinner and delivered a rant in front of customers.

His message was always the same.

"The fish smell. It's o-vah-whelming. My en-ty-ah family is lined up at the toilet, wretching."

And my message was always the same.

"Mr. Wurmtsch, I don't know what to tell you, we haven't gotten any other complaints.

"Our fish doesn't smell before we cook it. I don't know how it can smell when it's being cooked."

"Stinky," he said, "that's how it smells. Stinky. People call us 'The Fish House.' Nobody wants to play with my kids."

Mr. Wurmtusch called the Pollution Control Board. They came out. Their representatives stood on all four corners of our property and sniffed.

They tried to identify what Mr. Wurmtusch was smelling.

Soon they were sniffing multiple times weekly.

One day they sniffed and sniffed, on tippy toes.

One said, "Here, you smell that?"

The other came and sniffed.

"Yeah."

"You think that's it?"

He sniffed a few more times.

"No," he said, "I think that's Dunkin' Donuts across the street."

He massaged his chin.

"But it could be that Kentucky Fried Chicken over there."

Even so, the Pollution Control Board suggested I get a "scrubber."

"What's that?"

"A scrubber will filter the cooking smells through a combination of charcoal and water and you won't be able to smell anything."

"Can you smell anything now?" I said.

He stopped.

"Not really," admitted the man from the Pollution Control Board.

"But…" I said.

"But you gotta do something," he said.

"Because of Wurmtusch?"

He paused.

"Yeah."

I checked into a scrubber. It would cost thousands of dollars.

I told Pollution Control.

The guy was nice.

"I'm in a bind," he said. "I gotta give 'em something. Wurmtusch is all over my boss, and my boss is all over me. Pollution's starting to be a big thing now."

"Even imaginary pollution?"

He smiled.

"Yeah," he said. "Sometimes."

I decided to call the president of CHEEKY'S Fish Tacos and see if he'd run into this before.

Lester Kane was the living definition of a tycoon. Larger than life, both in personality and physical size.

The day I called CHEEKY'S headquarters in Miami, a man answered.

"Hi, this is Layng Martine up in Connecticut, who's this?"

"Hey, Layng, Jim Richards."

Jim was the CFO. Answering the phone?

"Hey, Jim, I thought I'd get Andrea."

"Yeah, we're kinda on skeleton crew down here, everybody doin' a little bitta everything."

"Where's Andrea?

"Gone."

"Gone?"

"Yeah, pretty much everybody's gone."

I digested that a moment.

"Harvey?"

"Yeah, Harvey, Mac, Ron, Lois, Big Bill Freeze, Carolyn, Jerry... pretty much everybody."

"Holy shit."

"Tell me about it."

"What's happening?"

"Tough times, good buddy, tough times."

"Jesus. Is Lester around?"

"Yeah, Lester we got."

"May I talk to him."

"Hold on a minute."

I stood out back of the restaurant and tapped my fingers on the dumpster until I heard a voice.

"Hey, Big Fella!!" It was Lester.

"Hey, Lester, what's going on down there?"

"Hell, if I knew that I'd be President." Pause. "Goddam...I AM President!!"

He laughed for 30 seconds.

"Lester, are you going down?"

"Shit no, we're not going down. We're in a lull, that's all. Just a lull. This get-rich-quick bullshit ain't a fucking snap like everybody thinks. It'll crunch your nuts, brotherdog, crunch your fucking nuts. But just when you think you can't take another twist on the ol' pecker…BOOM! Sunshine!!! I've been there, son, I wrote the fucking book!!!"

"Lester, I don't want to get rich quick, I want to stay alive."

"Spoken like the true genius I know you are."

"Lester, I've got a situation up here I've got to take care of."

"Shoot."

"Guy behind us claims we're making his house smell like fish, whole family's sick, calls five times a week. Now he's got the Pollution Control Board on us and I've got to do something. Something so they know I'm at least trying."

"Have you brought up the fact that our product don't smell?"

"Yes. Even the Pollution guys admit they can't identify the smell but this guy is driving them crazy. Their head man is leaning on my guy and now I've got to do something. I just don't know what. They want me to put in a scrubber. Thousands of dollars. Can't do that. You seen this before?"

"Seen a version of it."

"Any clues?"

Thoughtful pause.

"He's a psycho. You know that, right?"

"The guy behind me?"

"Yeah. Because there ain't no fucking smell from our fish."

"Right, but…"

"So we start with he's a nutcase and treat him like the fruitcake he is. That means…a show. He needs a show. You gotta show him you're busting your ass to get rid of the problem. Even though there ain't a fucking problem. Are you there?"

"I'm here."

"You gotta put a little tweet tweet up on the screen and make him think he's seen the right movie."

"Like what?"

"OK, lemme think about this a minute."

Two cars pulled into the parking lot.

That's good. Probably a few orders of fries and a couple of drinks. I'm assured of at least $7 for this hour's cash register reading.

Lester started talking.

"You got a good A/C guy?"

"Yes. I do."

"All right, here's what you do...first of all you gotta do it on a Saturday when Mr. Warmbutt..."

"Wurmtusch."

"What's the fucking difference? Like I say, Saturday. This ass-hole's gotta be home to see everything. You gotta have like a million guys in matching outfits running up and down ladders and hammering big shiny-ass air ducts and carrying mini-pipes and hoses and screaming shit like "Roger!! Turn on C-6!!."...you gotta shoot so much wind up his ass he thinks he's a hurry-cane."

"I like it."

"Damn straight. You do that for 8-10 hours he'll swear that fucking smell is gone."

"All right, let me call my guy."

Three days later, on a sunny spring Saturday, the circus pulled up to the restaurant.

Two vans, three ladders, six guys in matching green uniforms saying "JUS-RITE HEAT & AIR."

I found out later that four of them were kids from the contractor's cul de sac that he paid double overtime to look frantic.

They laid a ladder up the back and one on the side. Both eminently visible from the Wurmtusch yard.

I glanced over.

Oh, a neighbor's dream.

Mr. and Mrs. Wurmtusch just walked outside with coffee.

They walked to the edge of their terrace and stood transfixed at the scene unfolding before them.

"Get those charcoal filters up there first," the contractor yelled.

Two guys with long thick boxes inched up the ladders.

As soon as they stepped onto the roof, three others followed carrying sheaves of PVC pipe and copper tubing.

From the roof, somebody called down to the contractor.

"Frank, how many copies of the schematics we got?"

"Two, Eddie, one's taped to the main filter casing. Jimmy, you and Mark come down and get it up to Eddie."

Two kids came down and eased a large rectangle of gleaming aluminum out of the service van.

"You guys need a helper on that?" Eddie called down.

"Fuckin' A," one hollered, dropping the heavy piece like a hot rock and leaving it hanging halfway out of the van bed.

"Get it over by the building," Eddie called, "we'll winch it up."

On the roof, they set up a tripod with a pulley, sent the rope over the edge, cradled the giant piece and eased it up to the roof.

Three guys hustled it over next to Eddie.

"What is this fucking thing?," one kid said, out of breath as he set his end down.

Eddie looked at it.

Then he looked at the kid.

"Huh? We built it. Go get the rivet gun."

For the next hour the activity was furious.

Somebody went inside, hooked up water to flexible tubing and snaked it up through the fan vent over the fryers and out the duct on the roof.

Up on the roof, Eddie and two others slid the large aluminum rectangle over the existing air vent's opening and after firing a few practice rounds of 3/8-inch rivets in the air to great fanfare...

"Christ, Eddie, aim the goddam thing over the parking lot!"

Eddie started in on the large aluminum rectangle.

Bap!...Bap!...Bap!...Bap!...Bap! the rivets slammed into the metal flanges and joined the two large rectangles together.

Out of the corner of my eye I stole a look at Wurmtusch.

He was Bapping! his hand against his coffee cup with the sound of every rivet.

I turned the other way and had to smile.

By mid-afternoon, water was running steadily out of the shiny new rectangle. Several lengths of white PVC ran along the aluminum sides and curved into the opening. They appeared to be hooked up to a water source.

"Is that Thurmond valve ready to be activated?" Frank called from the middle of the parking lot.

"Thurmond valve?" I thought. "I love it."

"I think we're buttoned up, Frank," Eddie hollered back.

"All right. We're gonna start cooking," I said.

Inside the store we cranked up the fryers and dropped in some fish.

In a minute I walked outside.

Earlier in the day, Wurmtusch and his wife had set up folding chairs at the edge of their yard, next our parking lot.

They were still there. Now with their three kids.

Frank and Eddie were both on the roof. With the four others they clustered around the vent-opening in an impressive green huddle.

"You smell anything?" I called.

Frank said, "I don't smell nothing," he turned to his left, "You, Eddie?"

"Fresh as a frigging daisy where I am," Eddie yelled down.

I walked around the parking lot, sniffing in different places.

After a few minutes I walked over to the building and yelled up to the men.

"Hey," I said, "We did it!"

"I guess to hell you did," said Frank, "This system is three times what you need, for Christ's sake."

Those words echoed well to all interested parties.

The crew carried down scraps of tubing and excess materials.

Finally, they telescoped both ladders and fastened them on the van roofs.

I went in and got extra large Cokes for everybody.

The kids sat on the van tailgates. Frank and Eddie leaned against the wall.

"Helluva day," Frank said.

When I got a phone call and had to go inside, I passed near Wurmtusch and his family.

He was smiling.

"It's bettah," he said.

A month or so of glorious peace followed.

No phone calls.

No surprise tirades during dinner.

The Pollution Control guys came by to say thanks.

The former harassment had almost become a distant memory.

Then one week it rained three days straight.

People were edgy.

Gloom settled over the region.

The third night the phone rang during our dinner mini-crush.

I grabbed it and said, "Hello?"

There was a brief moment of silence before I heard a familiar voice.

"Mistuh Mahteen?" he said.

"Yes," I said.

"It's back."

CHAPTER 15

I saw Lester Kane, CHEEKY'S president, one last time before I went bankrupt.

It was a Sunday. I was in the bathtub crying when he called.

Linda was bringing me a cup of hot tea and the phone when she walked into the bathroom.

"It's Lester Kane," she said, passing the receiver to me in the tub.

Lester was the guy we still depended on.

Our Guru.

If anyone had answers, it was Lester.

"I'm coming up there Tuesday," he said, "we're having a meeting."

Lester flew up to a motel at LaGuardia Airport to conduct an afternoon pep talk for franchisees in the region.

All of us were hurting.

Most in dire straits.

Apparently, fish tacos were not destined to replace the hamburger as our national obsession after all.

There were eight franchisees around a fake wood table in the motel conference room.

Lester stood at one end.

He was 6'8".

His suit jacket was open. His silver belt buckle the size of a small hubcap.

Lester turned on his a ten-gallon smile, took a sip of water and scanned faces around the table.

"Don't look so worried!" he said, crushing his water cup and firing it into the waste basket, self-confidence bouncing off the walls.

Then he took off his jacket, hung it on the back of his chair, put on his game face, and started talking.

"I'm up here to help you guys solve problems," he said. "I want you to ask questions, nothing is off the table. If you've got a situation, chances are I've seen it, so shoot. Remember, I've got one goal, and that's to help you," here he stopped and made individual eye contact with each of one of us, "unnerstand? Help you solve problems, make money. So…who wants to go first?"

A hand shot up.

"Jerome," said Lester.

"Lester, my Sundays are weak. Almost nobody in the store. I'm thinking maybe Sundays I should close."

Lester looked down at the table, smiled, then looked up.

"Jerome," he said, "you can't expect much business on Sundays. It's the end of the weekend. People have blown their load Friday and Saturday. The kids are doing homework. What you're seeing is what every store is gonna see Sundays and you can't worry about it. You're not doing anything wrong…

Who else? Louis…"

"Yeah, Lester, I'm having trouble on Tuesday. I've tried promotions, Tuesday-only coupons, did a two-for-one with the high school. I get a little pump-up, but nothing sticks. Next week I'm back slow as ever."

"Well, Louis, Tuesday is Tuesday," said Lester, "the week's just getting started. A lot of people travel on their jobs early in the week. It's not close enough to Friday to start celebrating. Folks are hunkered down trying to make a living. What can I tell you? That's life. It's Tuesday, OK? Anybody else got a problem?"

Another hand shot up. Faraq.

"Lester, ever since I open I getting kill on Wednesday..."

"Faraq," said Lester, "before you say another word about Wednesday, think about where your store is. One of the most exclusive, one of the richest towns in the U.S. Of course you don't do any business on Wednesday, Faraq. Wednesday is the maid's night off. It's family night. Only night of the week the family can be alone, nobody in the wings, talk private business..."

All at once, from the other end of the table I heard a shout.

A little, round, beady-eyed guy was waving his hand, unable to contain himself.

"Lester!" he said, "Lester!!"

Lester stopped talking and slowly looked toward the excited voice...

"Yes, Jeffery."

"Lester, I'm very interested in this," his arms now spread wide, palms up.

"I'm glad you are."

"Yes," he said, "I'm very interested in this, because, I don't know about Miami where you are, Connecticut like him, or Long Island, New Jersey, wherever, but down in Philly where I'm at? We only got seven fucking nights in the week."

CHAPTER 16

One hour after leaving the motel conference room I was back in my apron at CHEEKY'S, overwhelmed by the feeling I had lost myself.

I wanted to be a songwriter. But instead, I had borrowed money, taken investors, and opened two of these places.

I was boxed-in, buried in debt. I had believed the brochures saying that these stores would never need me.

Instead they took every waking hour and even that was not enough.

They were losing money each minute and I had no idea how to stop the bleeding.

I thought back to the day I had walked into the Turf Bar with the song I'd made up.

I remembered how afraid I was, pacing up and down outside on the sidewalk.

And I remembered the helpless passion that drove me to reach for the door and go in.

I still had it.

My reverie was broken by the smack of a teenager's palm on the door to the restaurant.

Outside I saw his bike leaning against the building.

"One order of fries, please," he said.

It was 3 p.m. The slowest part of the day.

The kid went to the ketchup dispenser, popped a few squirts on his fries and took them to one of our inside picnic-style tables.

We didn't have another customer that day until 4:30.

"Tomorrow I'm not coming in here," I thought. "I'm going to New York."

The next day someone took my shift at the restaurant and I took the train into The City.

David Rosner was an important music publisher. He had been a friend for six years.

We first met back when I was in college taking songs to FGG Productions.

Later on, David had been running CBS' music publishing entities during my time there.

Now he was running another major music publishing company.

David's large office was on a high floor.

He hadn't known I was coming but he made time for me.

I flopped down in a chair facing him at his desk.

"I can't get music out of my blood," I said.

David smiled.

"Why am I not surprised?" he said, with the good nature of a big brother, or maybe a kind father.

"I'm dying out there," I said. "I'm meant to write songs but I don't have a minute to think of anything but how I'm going to pay the food supplier, which kid didn't show up for work, which A/C system will quit working today."

David looked at me.

"What do you want?" he said.

"I need a 'home'," I said, "a home for my songs. I need a publisher where I can write any kind of song I want — funny, sad, fast, slow, country, rock, anything — and the guy running the company will get it. Maybe someone who produces records, too…but where the hell is that guy?"

"What about the restaurants?"

"Right now I need them to survive," I said, "but I've got to find a way out, throw everything into music."

David listened.

After a minute or two he said, "What about Ray Stevens?"

I looked at David…and sat back fast in my chair.

That was a breakthrough.

I knew Ray as a songwriter, record producer and Grammy-winning singer of songs of every stripe. Very funny, very serious, fast, slow, influences in rock, gospel, country. Nothing seemed out of his grasp.

"God," I said, "that's an incredible idea."

Minutes later I was on a pay phone outside David's building on Broadway getting the number for Ray Stevens' Nashville office.

The woman who answered Ray's phone had a gentle Southern accent and sounded like someone I might've known all my life.

I gave her my name and asked if she thought Ray would be in town for the next few days.

"Yes," she said, "as far as I know he's here until Friday."

"Thank you," I said, "may I ask your name?"

"Ann."

The next morning instead of driving to the restaurant, I left my employees in charge. I drove to LaGuardia Airport and flew to Nashville where I took my guitar and a taxi to the small bungalow that was Ray's office on Nashville's Music Row, center of Nashville's music business.

I got out of the cab and stood looking at the small house.

No sign. Just the number by the front door: 1009.

Really? This huge star in this simple place?

I didn't know that all of Music Row was once residential. These houses that still looked like homes had been re-zoned for offices and were now filled daily with most of the people and businesses that powered the Nashville music industry.

I walked up two steps to the porch, opened the door and went in.

A smiling red-haired woman sat at a desk facing me.

"Ann?" I said.

"Yes."

"Hi, I'm Layng Martine Jr., I called yesterday?"

"Yes, I remember. You didn't waste any time."

I smiled at the surprising welcome.

"No, you're right. I guess I'm excited." I paused before broaching the question, "Ann, is there any chance of seeing Ray for a few minutes? I'm a writer...I have two or three songs I'd like to play him."

From the other room came a voice.

"How long ya here for?"

I looked left. A burly, smiling face sat at another desk, sporting a distinct New York manner and accent.

"Well," I said, "I just came to see Ray, so I guess I'm leaving after I see him."

"Where ya from?"

"Connecticut."

"Yeah? My brother lives in Connecticut."

"Really...?"

"Yeah. He's crazy. Goes into New York every day on a train. What a life...You a singer?"

"A little bit...more a songwriter. Right now I just want to get going. I'll do anything."

He looked at Ann.

"Lemme see what Ray's doing," he said to both of us, got up from his desk and disappeared.

"That's Mike," Ann said, "he's the radio promotion guy for Ray's records."

Mike had a booming voice.

A few seconds later I heard it bounce up the hallway from a back room.

"Hey, Raymone," I heard Mike say, "kid's out there, came down here today from Connecticut to see you...I got a feeling about this guy."

A minute or two later Mike reappeared and leaned in the doorway between the two rooms.

"Hang around half hour or so and you can see Ray."

"Thank you," I said, looking at both Ann and Mike, "I appreciate that so much."

Ray Stevens had had a TV show the past summer, the summer replacement for "The Andy Williams Show." I had watched it and remember thinking he didn't look much older than me.

Minutes later I heard footsteps in the hall behind Ann's desk and Ray came into the room. Slim, dark hair, glasses, about 5'11" and smiling. Every bit the warm person I'd seen on TV.

I felt instantly at home.

"Hi," he said, "I'm Ray Stevens."

"Layng Martine Jr.," I said.

"That's quite a name," he said, with a mischievous lift of the eyebrows.

"Yep," I said, "I'm stuck with it."

"Heck, no," he said, "that's a *good* thing."

Back in his small office Ray sat down on a chair and I found a spot opposite him on a loveseat.

"Whaddaya got?" he said.

"A few songs..."

He tapped his fingers on the arm of the chair.

"Let's hear'em."

I unzipped my guitar case, checked the tuning, and played my first song.

"Not bad," he said, adjusting his glasses, "what else ya got?"

After the third song he said, "That sounds commercial to me."

I played two more and stopped.

"What are you looking to do?" said Ray.

"Anything," I said, "I want to get started. I want a career in music, writing songs..."

Ray interrupted.

"You sing pretty good," he said, "I like that one song a lot. I think it could be a hit."

I froze in my seat. Did I just hear what I thought I heard?

"Well, thank you..."

"You wanting to be a singer?"

"Sure..." I said.

When I said I'd do "anything," I meant it.

Life writing ads or behind the counter of my fish tacos place was not even close to the way I wanted to live.

Ray wiggled his nose a few times under his glasses.

"If you write me another song as good as that one I like, I'll record you."

I flew back to New York on a magic carpet.

A great feeling of hope washed all over me.

This was going to work. I believed that finally I was onto something that might actually lead to the kind of life I dreamed of: doing what I loved and earning a living at it. The best kind of freedom.

I got home and wrote songs in a fury. Week after week I completed new ones and sent them to Nashville for Ray to hear.

Long distance phone calls were expensive in those days. Ray devised an arrangement that would put the cost of our calls on him. I would call his office "person-to-person," a service the phone company used to provide back when calls were so costly and you didn't want to pay if the person you were calling wasn't there.

In the system Ray came up with, the operator would ask for "Layng Martine Jr.," Ann would say "He's not here," then she'd tell Ray I called and he'd call me back.

This went on for months.

I'd mail Ray a cassette of a new song, wait a few days, then call to see what he thought of it.

"Not sure about this one," he'd say, or "Sounds like a good 'B' side," or "Almost, almost."

Nine months went by.

It was springtime and my day off from the restaurant. A group of us were in our next door neighbors' backyard. Our 2-year-old son Layngo and his buddies splashed in a plastic wading pool. We grilled burgers and lay in the sun.

I was strumming my guitar.

Someone asked her husband to put suntan lotion on her back.

"Rub it in," she said.

"Rub it in, rub it in," I strummed idly on my guitar, putting the phrase to a simple melody.

Linda lifted up her head.

"Is that already a song?" she said.

"I don't think so…" I answered.

"Sounds like a hit," she said, closing her eyes and lying back down.

"Yeah, it does," somebody else chimed in.

I kept on playing, gradually adding words around a simple story:

"Lay beside me on the sand

Put some lotion on your hand…"

By the end of the day the song had taken shape.

By early evening we'd come inside and were sitting at our friends' kitchen table.

"Is the song finished?" asked Madeline, our longtime friend.

"No," I said, "not quite. It needs a middle."

"Like what?"

And then something happened that only happens once in a while. The entire middle of the song, melody and all, appeared in my head.

"Like," I said, "Put a little on my nose, put a little on my toes, put it on my back and my sacroiliac and a dab on my chinny chin chin, rub it in, rub it in…"

"That's fantastic!" everybody said.

"Jesus," I said, "it does sound great...," as astounded as the others.

That night I sang "Rub It In" into my cassette player and first thing the next morning mailed the tape to Nashville.

Four days later I was serving a Thursday lunch rush at the restaurant when the phone rang. I grabbed the receiver and tucked it up to my ear with my hunched shoulder as I made change and handed it to a customer.

"CHEEKY'S Fish Tacos," I said.

Suddenly, I heard a familiar voice.

"Layng?" said Ray Stevens.

"Yes, Ray, hi..."

"'Rub It In' is a smash, we're gonna record. When can you get down here?"

My heart rate tripled.

"You name it," I said, abandoning my post at the cash register and disappearing into the back by the walk-in freezer.

Ten days later I was standing at a microphone in Jack Clement's renowned Nashville recording studio where Charley Pride, Kris Krisofferson, Bobby Bare and many others had recorded huge hits.

I'm surrounded by musicians.

Everyone in the room but me was famous.

Every instrument was manned by someone who'd played on a lifetime of hit records...many of which, if not most, I owned.

The studio itself was made to feel like a cabin in the woods, anchored by a small wood-shingled "porch" with roof over it where the drums were set up.

Everything about the room was homey.

The banter back and forth between the musicians was relaxed, full of kidding and humor.

When one of the guitar players suggested an interesting riff for a song's introduction, somebody said "Hey, isn't that the lick you played this morning on the Waylon Jennings session?"

Much laughter.

But when the red "Record" light went on, they were all business.

I don't think I ever had to play my new songs for them more than once before they had chord charts completed. They could play the songs more or less perfectly even though they'd first heard them just a moment ago.

When the three-hour session was over it was 5 p.m.

"I think we cut two today," said drummer Jerry Carrigan. He meant two hits.

Ray swiveled in his chair to face Jerry and popped his palm on the wooden counter next to the recording console.

"I think you're right, man!" he said.

They were talking about my songs, my records.

Except for seeing my wife and son for the first time...to date I'd had no feeling in my life that could touch this one.

The next day I flew back home and waited.

For the next weeks, Ray was back in the studio adding an instrument or two on the songs, personally adding his own brilliant background parts to my vocals and eventually mixing all the tracks together to make a final record.

Occasionally, we'd talk.

"'Rub It In' is coming hard," he said at one point.

"You mean making it all gel?"

"Yeah," he said, "but we'll get it."

I went back to work cooking fish, imploring purveyors to deliver even though I was behind on their bills, and hassling with the garbage company who'd installed a dumpster half the size of our miniscule parking lot, eliminating three of our nine parking spaces.

My comfort was knowing that while I went about these mind-numbing tasks, a genius was back in Nashville bringing my songs to life.

"Rub It In" was released as a single on August 12, 1971.

And, as it turned out, my version of it *was* a hit. Unfortunately, it was only a hit in a few cities because by the time it had proven itself and was ready to spread elsewhere, summer was over, and a song about suntan lotion and the beach didn't line up with the onslaught of chilly days and fall weather.

But "Rub It In" had worked magic on me. It proved to me that I could write a hit song.

Meanwhile, the restaurants were crashing around me. The cash squeeze was constant. Nearly every day I had to beg our food supplier to hang with me when my checks bounced and I was already a week behind. Now he was demanding cash. No more checks. That meant I couldn't pay the rent on time and was sometimes late in paying my employees.

Twice a week I had to meet the delivery truck at 6 a.m. with a brown bag full of cash.

I had to get out.

Linda and I talked it over.

Mixed in our discussion was the question, "Do I go back into advertising, the safer route, or shoot for our dreams in Nashville?"

Typical of the guts shown by Linda in all decisions both before and after that day was her simple response.

"Nashville," she said, "no choice."

We set a new course.

The first step was easy.

The real estate taxes on one store were raised so high it was the last straw.

I closed it.

It was quickly re-opened by two guys who had been my customers.

I concentrated on selling the one remaining store.

The two guys who had taken over the first store wanted this one, too.

After weeks of back and forth between our lawyers we reached an agreement.

They would take over my lease, all obligations to suppliers, and the remaining payments on equipment.

We scheduled a closing.

Linda was nine months pregnant with our second child. Due any day.

The thought of the restaurants being off our backs was a giant relief.

We were counting the minutes.

Our house was on the market, too.

When a buyer for it came quickly, another huge weight lifted.

Two days before the closing on the restaurant, mentally it was already sold.

We felt free.

Poor, but free.

I was at home doing the payroll on the kitchen table.

Behind me, the phone rang.

I grabbed it.

"Layng, it's Joanne, the restaurant is on fire...before you say anything...yes, I called the fire department. They're coming."

I stood up.

"How?" I said, "How serious? Are you in the store?"

"Yes, I'm in the back. Charles poured peanut oil into the empty fryer and forgot it was already on 'high' so the oil exploded and set the ceiling on fire."

"Fire extinguisher?"

"Flames are too hot. Can't get close enough to spray..."

"Get out of there and wait for the fire department."

"OK."

"I'm leaving now," I said, "I'll be there."

I hung up the phone and turned to Linda.

"I think I just felt a contraction," she said.

"How long ago?"

"A minute or two."

"Think we should go to the hospital?"

"No. Let's see how far apart they are. What happened at CHEEKY'S?"

"Kid poured oil in the fryer, forgot it was on. Oil flared up and caught the ceiling tiles on fire...Fire Department's coming."

"You go."

"Let's wait for a few more contractions."

Linda sat down in the kitchen. I started a new pot of coffee.

Ten minutes later another contraction.

"It's going to be hours," she said. "You go. Your mom can drive me to the hospital if they get close."

"You think hours?"

"Yes. Go ahead."

The drive to CHEEKY'S was 40 minutes.

When I got there the fire department had left.

Flames had licked up through the front windows of the building and left black stripes across the facade.

Three kids, my employees, stood talking in the parking lot.

The front door hung wide open.

The front windows had been smashed out.

I walked inside.

Wet, still-smouldering ceiling tiles drooped over the cash register and sat scattered on the floor and counter. They covered the cooking area in blackened squares and filled the room with the rancid smell of smoke and burn. Water was everywhere. Insulation dripped through the rafters like Spanish moss.

The walls were charred and scarred and the tables and benches tipped over.

"The buyers will walk," I thought as I stood in the wreckage.

Clearly the firemen's mission had been, "Put out the fire and leave."

Understandable.

I called a carpenter to board up the windows, asked one of the kids to stay till it was done, and shot for home to see about Linda and the baby.

Midway I stopped at a payphone.

No answer at home.

No answer at my mom's.

Reached my sister who said Linda had just driven herself to the hospital.

Thirty minutes later I was there.

I screeched into the drop-off circle, parked, and ran to an elevator.

Linda was in the last throes of labor. Her face was red and strained. She smiled when she saw me and I took her hand.

"I guess the second one really does come faster," she said between breaths.

An hour later, out slipped a beautifully healthy Tucker Martine.

I called Linda's parents. Her dad answered.

When I said, "His name is Tucker," I thought I felt a slight pause.

It was only much later we realized we could've named him Joe, after Linda's dad.

That would've been a great name, too.

When the nurse brought Tucker to Linda's room and handed him to her wrapped in a tiny blue blanket, our 2-and-a-half-year-old son Layngo stood wide-eyed.

"My brother?" he whispered, looking up at me and holding onto my leg.

"Yes," I said.

He looked back at the soft blue lump Linda held to her chest.

"He's small," he said.

Everybody laughed.

While our families talked I went to a pay phone and called the carpenter who had boarded up the store.

"You won't be back in there for a while," he said.

"How long, you think?"

"Three months? Ya gotta gut the place…"

I hung up and wondered if the buyers would wait that long. Seemed unlikely.

It was.

The next morning they called to say they were out.

I went back to the room.

New faces had arrived. Party mood had taken over.

Somebody had champagne and was filling small paper cups for everyone.

Tucker was in Linda's arms and my sister was taking pictures.

"He looks like Linda," someone said.

"He's lucky," said my brother.

Laughs.

The nurse came and took Tucker back to the nursery.

Linda needed a rest.

A bunch of us walked to an Italian restaurant for dinner.

Nobody knew about the fire.

And I wasn't bringing it up.

The mood was festive. Many toasts to Tucker and Layngo and Linda and me.

"Such a wonderful day," Linda's mom said raising her glass, looking at me, "now you have two beautiful boys. What could be better than that?"

"Absolutely nothing," I said.

We all clinked glasses and stayed up too late.

That night Layngo slept in Linda's place on our king-size bed and we fell asleep holding hands.

When I woke up he was still sleeping.

His tiny arm was wrapped around my shoulder.

I lay there for a few extra minutes because that morning I needed somebody's arm around me and none was better than his.

Then I woke him up and took him to nursery school.

CHAPTER 17

——————

Two days after Tucker was born we brought him home.

Linda set up a self-swinging baby seat in our living room and began to pack for Nashville.

The morning of the closing on the sale of our house it snowed.

My mom watched Tucker while Linda and I went to the lawyer's office.

After the papers were signed, Linda went home.

I walked up the snow-dusted sidewalk a few blocks to the bank from which I'd borrowed money to buy CHEEKY'S.

I did what I thought was the right thing.

I told them my business had failed, that we were moving to Nashville, and gave them our new address.

Then I made a mistake that would teach me a lesson I would never forget.

I deposited $12,000 of the $14,000 proceeds from the sale of our house in that bank.

My plan was to leave our savings there and withdraw it as needed for living or to buy another house.

As agreed, I was paying interest-only on the loan and had never missed a payment.

But I would never see that money again.

A few months after we moved to Nashville I tried to withdraw cash toward living expenses. I was told I could have an additional $2,000 but that since I had moved out of state, was unemployed, and my loan balance for the CHEEKY'S purchase was greater than the balance of our savings account, I was no longer considered a wise risk and therefore no further withdrawals would be permitted.

Suddenly, I was in a new city with a wife, two kids, no cash, and cut off from the money we thought we had.

I asked Ray Stevens if he could advance me $200 a week against my future royalties. He did, even though whether or not I'd ever earn any royalties was an utter unknown. We agreed that any money the songs did earn would be split down the middle: mine the "writer's share," his the "publisher's share." My share would go to him until the advances were repaid. Traditional, and very fair.

To make ends meet Linda sewed beautiful patchwork designs on denim workshirts. People saw me wearing them and wanted one. I took and delivered orders. She sold a lot of those shirts and we needed every nickel she made.

I managed to suppress the thought that a 29-year-old guy with a family should be a little more advanced in life than this.

To supplement my draw from Ray Stevens I got night and weekend jobs as a bartender. I painted walls and radiators. For $75 I once dressed-up like a fudgecake with a beachball for a cherry on my head to be in a Shoney's Big Boy commercial, and I regularly loaded trucks at night for UPS and, as a member of the Teamsters Union, for Roadway Express.

On my first night at Roadway, I reported to work early for the 12:30 a.m. shift, so I decided to locate the break room. When I opened the door, two men about 40 years old had another guy up against the candy machine. All three of them were laughing. In the scramble, one of the two giggling aggressors hollered, "GRAB EEZ BALLS!"

It was a far cry from my 17th floor office on Madison Avenue.

But I had chosen this, and I knew it. I'm now reminded of a day years later when legendary songwriter Harlan Howard ("I Fall To Pieces"), after listening to a long tale of woe from a struggling young songwriter on the next barstool, slowly looked over at the boy.

"Son," the great man said, "did anybody send for you?"

No one had sent for me. No one had forced me to leave my cushy advertising job for this unpredictable journey. Loading trucks, eating a bag lunch at 4:30 a.m. in that break room, was a way to keep going while I tried to succeed at what I loved. Membership in the Teamsters Union was hard to come by. The pay was good. I had great respect for the job.

Even to some close friends, the nitty-gritty of trying to earn a living while writing songs was unfamiliar.

At a neighbor's festive gathering one Thanksgiving, with Linda and me and our boys all dressed up and the turkey, flowers and beautiful plates of stuffing and vegetables on the table, I had to leave the party mid-meal and head for the loading docks at Roadway.

Much as I hated to go, my shift was about to start and my leaving seemed totally normal to me.

But a baffled guest said, "Why are you doing that truck job, Layng? You've already written enough songs for the rest of your life."

"I know," I said, gently as possible, "but none of them have made any money."

And I had no idea if they ever would.

Sometimes I thought that if one of my songs became a hit that I would have everything. And that thought scared me a little because I knew that no one ever gets everything.

As much faith as I had in the songs I was turning out, many nights when I was inside an oven- hot trailer pulling down a roll of carpet, hoping one of my songs would be successful, I'd stop short

204 —   LAYNG MARTINE JR.

and think, "Wait a minute, how realistic is it in this life that I can have Linda...AND a hit record?"

Often, it seemed too much to ask.

As consumed as I was by songwriting, the fish tacos debacle was still close enough behind to reach out and grab us.

The Country Cottage was a restaurant in an old house serving simple country food.

Linda and I met there for lunch one day and she brought a letter from the company that had financed the equipment for the burned restaurant.

With late fees and penalties, the original balance had now tripled. By coincidence, days later, the bank back in Connecticut returned my latest interest payment with a letter saying that interest-only was no longer good enough, I must begin paying principal.

I was already working two jobs and barely able to make ends meet. There was no more money.

And there were no more hours in the day to work.

A friend recommended a lawyer and I went to see her about declaring bankruptcy.

"How much do you owe?" she asked.

I told her.

"What's the value of your assets?"

I told her.

"How much do you make a week?"

I told her.

"Well," she smiled, "you're definitely bankrupt."

I had to smile, too.

Then I looked at her.

"What are the ramifications?" I said.

"Not much. Clean slate. You start over. You don't have anything, but you don't owe anybody."

"Could we ever buy a house if we get going again?"

"Yes. Some banks will consider you an even better risk since you can only declare bankruptcy every seven years."

I processed that.

"Crazy," I said.

"Yeah."

"What can we keep?"

"$1,250 worth of property."

"Including car?"

"Including anything."

I thought about it for a few days. The idea of not paying people, even the company that had unfairly inflated my original debt, felt awful.

But as I thought about trying to keep our family going while sending even a few dollars monthly to repay these soaring obligations, the decision made itself.

It was chilly and gray the morning Linda and I walked into bankruptcy court in Nashville and took our seats in a courtroom packed with other moms and dads and mostly respectable-looking souls who had also found themselves hopelessly buried in debt.

We each listened as our names were read and our liabilities discharged forever.

The readings took about an hour.

Suddenly at the sound of a voice and a gavel the legal proceedings were over.

People sat for a moment, unsure what to do.

Then, in the silence, someone got up.

Others rose and moved toward the aisles and the door.

One or two strangers quietly said hello to each other.

The fresh air hit our faces and we buttoned up our coats.

Suddenly, we were free to start again.

We had two battered cars and our furniture, which was mostly porch furniture.

The $66 remaining in our checking account was swept out the next morning by the U. S. government.

Twenty-two months after arriving in Nashville, Linda and I drove home from the courthouse and never looked back.

I wrote songs like a madman.

In one three-month period I wrote 43 new songs. Of course, the hope was that one or two of them would be great, but there was another motivation: Having a new song to play Ray Stevens was the only way to get his critique and feedback and thereby learn to improve as a songwriter. So, new song = new songwriting lesson.

For 10 or 20 seconds after playing him a new song Ray would say his piece.

It was usually a simple sentence or two, like: "you lost me in that third line" or "not enough of an idea to write a song about" or "chorus needs to be longer." Occasionally it was just hunched shoulders and a blank stare that said "what can I tell ya?"

Much as it hurt sometimes, Ray's clear, quick critique was priceless.

Once in a while he'd say, "That's a smash," and when he did, no matter how many turn-downs the song got I never stopped believing.

Soon I got better at anticipating what Ray would say and could often make the changes myself.

That was the "lessons" and critiques paying off.

Our agreement was that Ray was my teacher, my coach, and often my introduction to people I didn't know. But not my songplugger.

A songplugger is the person who takes a song out into the marketplace in hopes of getting it recorded. I didn't need someone to do that, I'd learn to do it myself. And, as it turned out, I loved it. I liked not having to depend on someone else to get my songs out there. And I liked the process of being in the room when a record producer or recording artist listened to my song. There's no feeling quite like seeing someone's eyes light up as a song plays...or having them turn one off after 15 seconds saying, "Wrong tempo."

In either case, you're at the source. You learn what people like, what they're after. It's my job to bring them something they need, and if they don't need it and they know that right away, why listen further?

Usually the listener will just hand back a song they reject, without comment.

But not always.

Once in while you pick up a nugget that helps fine-tune your next pitch. A nugget like, "You know she just had a miscarriage, I don't think she'll be singing about kids for a while."

Things you mightn't learn if not there in person.

A thick skin helps. And a sense of humor.

One day I took songs to a friend at a large record company. She was looking for material for her long roster of artists.

She listened to my first song.

When it finished playing she looked across the desk and said, "Wow, Layng, that's...I don't HATE it...I mean I usually love your songs, but...not that one...got something else?"

"Yes," I said.

She took my second CD, slid it in the player, swiveled around in her chair, faced the wall and listened. When it was finished she turned back around and paused, and without a hint of irony said, "to be honest, I liked the first one better."

Almost right away, alongside my new songs, I began pitching my version of "Rub It In" as a demo.

Elvis was my first idea. It seemed "perfect" for him, as had my first song "Swagger" years before.

I sent "Rub It In" off to the address I had for Elvis, but heard nothing.

I played it for many producers with no takers.

Few thought it was a song that fit any Nashville artists.

Then a new idea surfaced.

A young guy named Billy "Crash" Craddock sang in an Elvis-y style and had a huge following among females. His records were more rock-oriented than most in country and they were reaching #1. "Rub It In" felt like a great match for "Crash."

Two days later I sat in the office of Crash's producer, Ron Chancey, played him "Rub It In" and three other songs.

Ron listened to each demo all the way through.

When the last one finished he looked across his desk and, as casually as if he were ordering a double-cheeseburger said, "We'll probably cut two of those."

I walked out of there with the blood so rushed-up in my head that it's a wonder I made it down the front steps without falling. Here was a guy who was cutting hits on a big-deal recording artist, a producer who'd been around a while who really knew what he was doing...and he loved two of my songs.

I thought about Linda, and I thought about our two little boys.

Maybe it was going to happen for us.

Several weeks later, I ran into Johnny Christopher, one of the finest rhythm guitar players who ever lived.

"Layng," he said, "we cut 'Rub It In' on Crash last night. It's a smash! Wait'll you hear the high steel part Lloyd Green put on in the chorus!"

Serendipitous info like this was often the way writers found out something good had happened...news that was especially mean-ingful because even though a producer might love a song when you play it for them, even intend to record it, for assorted reasons it often doesn't actually make it to the recording session.

A songwriter maxim in the pre-CD era was, "It ain't final til it's vinyl."

We all attempted to live by those words and allow in just enough hope to keep us going...but not enough to crush us when a possi-bility evaporated.

"Rub It In" by Billy "Crash" Craddock was released as a single in April 1974. It took off in Texas and spread quickly across the states and up the *Billboard* Country Chart, where it reached #1, and then onto the Pop and Adult Contemporary Charts.

But, I was still loading trucks at Roadway because it takes nine months to a year before money from a hit song starts coming in.

Suddenly, the advertising business from which I had bolted three years before jumped back into my life in the most wonderful way.

One morning I was at Ray Stevens' publishing company writing when I got a phone call from Toni Wine, one of the most successful jingle singers who ever lived. She was at a studio up the street recording a Kentucky Fried Chicken commercial. One of her scheduled background singers had failed to show up.

"Can you come over and sing his part?"

Are you kidding?

"I'm on my way."

Since I'm a slow-study on harmony parts she gave me the lead melody to sing on the jingle. I already knew the melody because different versions of the jingle had been all over TV and radio for years. The words were "Hey, it's a, Kentucky Fried Chicken Day."

A few weeks after that hour or so I'd spent in the studio singing the jingle, I started getting checks in the mail from it being played on the radio. The checks would be for odd, relatively small amounts...$34.12, $71.26, $21.03. But they kept coming every few days from a company in Chicago called Talent & Residuals. The first three or four checks we just spent, treating them as "pennies from heaven," never dreaming they would continue. But they did. Since I was taking home about $50 a night for knocking myself out loading trucks and missing plenty of time with Linda and our boys while doing so, by about the fifth check we sat down to talk about this unexpected windfall.

"I could stop loading trucks and be with you guys more," I said, "but if we start banking the money we might build up toward the down payment on a house."

"We should save the money," Linda said. "If you quit loading trucks and the checks stop tomorrow, we've got a problem."

"Exactly."

I continued loading trucks and the checks kept on coming until we had saved a bit over $2,500. And then the checks did stop.

But in Nashville, at that time, $2,500 was enough for us to put down on a small two-family house.

Linda spotted one, buried in weeds but with "good bones" and in a good location.

It was $27,500.

We bought it.

Linda and I cut the weeds, greened-up the lawn, painted the house inside and out ourselves, and thought it was the coolest little place on the planet.

Our mortgage payment with taxes and insurance was $223 a month. The rent from the tiny second floor apartment we leased out was $125, which meant we only had to come up with $98 monthly for housing. Since the rent we had paid for our first Nashville apartment was $215, we were now reducing expenses, going in the right direction. Suddenly we had extra money. We could go to movies, sometimes take the kids to a place called Shakey's Pizza and to McDonald's.

Our small house had a great fireplace and some nights I'd build a fire, put on a record, and fall asleep by the hearth listening to Don Williams or Ray Charles.

Two years from bankruptcy our confidence was rising and for the first time in years we had a sense of security.

About this time, Ray gave me an office.

Actually, I asked for it.

It had been a broom closet. Four feet by four feet.

"You want to be in that little space?"

"Yes."

"Well," he said, blinking his eyes and shaking his head, "it's yours."

I thought I'd died and gone to heaven.

I told Linda and all our friends that, now, I have an office.

A buddy picked me up for lunch soon after I'd moved in.

He opened the door and found me in there playing my guitar into a tape player.

"What's this?" he said.

"It's my office."

"Office? It looks like a broom closet."

"Well, it was a broom closet. Now it's my office. Do you have an office?"

"No."

I opened my hands, smiled, and lifted my eyebrows.

"I have an office."

I wrote a lot of songs that changed our family's life in that tiny room, including a song called "Way Down" which later became very important to me and to us.

What inspired "Way Down" and the other songs I wrote one after another in that precious space was a combination of the music stirring wildly inside me, and fear.

Fear that if I wasn't successful I wouldn't be able to support my family.

The quest for a hit idea was always on.

In one unforgettable moment, a friend and I sat on the floor of his apartment and rapid-fire spat out the most inane and free-association song titles we could think of. All have long since disappeared from memory. Except for one. On one of my turns I said, "Don't Boogie Woogie When You Say Your Prayers Tonight"... both of us stopped short, "THAT'S A SMASH!" we said in virtual unison. And eventually, after being a minor chart record for Jerry Lee Lewis in America, it did become a smash...in France...as translated into "Pas De Boogie Woogie" by French star Eddy Mitchell.

Most of the songs written during those years are a blur of energy with few recollections of the actual writing process.

It's only in retrospect I noticed that three of the songs that helped build our economic base contained forms of onomatopoeia: "Rub It In," "Wiggle Wiggle," and "Way Down." In each case the rhythms and melodies "rubbed" and "wiggled" and went "way down" right along with the lyrics.

I had…and still have…notebooks filled with possible song titles. When a word or phrase struck me as a good title I'd write it on a scrap of paper, put the scrap in the left rear pocket of my jeans and every few days transpose the collected ideas into a notebook.

Every morning I'd go into my office and if I was stuck for an idea I'd flip through my notebooks.

"Way Down" may have popped out like that.

What I remember about "Way Down" is that when I played it for Ray Stevens he liked it right away and said, "Hey, there's nothing much going on around here today, let's call the band and demo this thing."

On the demo, I sang the lead, Ray played the piano and sang the bass part, which was such a grabber, such a memorable "hook."

With so much pounding and wailing coming out of that broom closet as I sang, strummed, and foot-stomped my way to a new song, I look back and wonder how Ray and his assistant, Shirley, stood the noise. My tiny space was only a few feet from their desks.

Sometimes while I was hacking away at an obvious loser I wonder if they were tempted to holler, "Please! No more! You're killing us!"

But they never did.

CHAPTER 18

The spring after "Rub It In" by Crash Craddock reached #1, I got my first royalty check.

Linda and I took our two boys to Disney World. We stayed at the Polynesian Village, brand new at the time. The swimming pool, with its manmade rocks and slides was right out our door. The bath towels in our room were thicker than the pillows we had at home.

We felt rich.

And compared to where we'd been, we were.

I told Ray Stevens that I owed it to him.

I still feel that way.

He had taught me.

He had opened doors.

He had backed me financially so that I could keep going when we had nothing.

Any suggestions he had, I took.

Except for one…and I would have taken that one if I'd been able to afford it. He was right.

It was during the late 70's huge run-up in the price of gold. The world had come unglued. Iran had taken 66 U.S. Citizens hostage. Threats to America seemed to be everywhere.

"Did you buy gold yet?" Ray said.

Apart from being a musical genius, Ray was also a business wizard.

He owned half the real estate in the city.

He owned copyrights, stocks, cash, the gamut.

About that time, I saw somebody at my bank slide open a deep, wide drawer of new Krugerrands and I felt as though someone were holding me up by the collar, above a land of golden skyscrapers.

A few days later Ray and I bumped into each other in the hallway of his office building.

"Did you buy gold yet?"…the question repeated in my head.

I was afraid he'd ask that.

"No," I said, "I haven't."

He stared at me like I was deaf.

"Layng," he said, "don't you read the papers? The world's a mess…things could boil over…"

Gold's rapidly rising price was part of every newscast.

People were scared.

Especially people with something to lose.

There was talk of the dollar being worthless and the need for every family to have a stash of precious metal in case all hell broke loose and gold or silver was all anyone would take in trade.

"Ray," I said, "gold is $400 an ounce. I can't afford that."

"One ounce?"

"Not really," I said. "That's a lot of money to me."

He thought about that for a second.

"You don't have $400?"

"I do, but…"

"Then buy silver," he said. "I'm just telling you…you gotta have something. Besides money."

I went back to my office.

"Am I crazy?" I thought.

I pictured my wife, and now our three kids. Was I failing to protect my family?

I called a local coin shop.

"Dimes and quarters," the man said, "that's how you buy silver in small amounts. Pre-1965 dimes and quarters."

"How much is silver per ounce?"

"Spot today is…$31.21 an ounce."

"How many dimes in an ounce?"

"About 11."

I hung up the phone.

Got out pen and pencil.

A hundred dollars would get me about 33 silver dimes.

I forgot about it.

A few days later I was in the office of a wealthy friend when his secretary called out, "Jamison Johns is on line three with an alert…"

Jamison Johns was the gold guru of the moment.

My friend snatched up the phone and listened for 90 seconds then slammed down the receiver.

"Rebecca," he hollered, "gold's going crazy."

I felt my blood pressure rise.

My friend stared at me across his desk.

He knew I was not a gold-owner.

"Layng," he said, "let me ask you something. If the Russians come across the Kentucky border, what are you going to give them for a loaf of bread…a dollar?"

"The Russians?" I said.

"Well," he said, "who knows?"

My mind was spinning.

Five minutes later there was a pounding on the back door of the building.

My friend was in the bathroom so I went toward the sound and opened the door.

I was facing a dolly stacked with large cardboard boxes marked "Third National Bank."

"Delivery for Mr. Roland," said the man behind the dolly.

I found my friend.

"Jimmy," I said, "there's a delivery out back from Third National Bank."

Jimmy stopped in his tracks.

"Now?" he said.

"Yes."

His eyes widened.

"My pennies!" he hollered.

Then he bolted for the door.

Apparently, copper was to be the next precious metal to "go crazy."

The delivery man stacked case after case of pennies in the center of the office lounge.

Jimmy watched as the island of tan rectangles grew.

Soon they took up most of the room's floor space.

Then the last carton was lifted into place, the dolly was rolled out of the building, and the back door to the building slammed shut.

Silence.

Suddenly Jimmy popped his palm on top of the cases and looked at me.

"Pennies, Layng, pennies" he said. "Can you afford a hundred dollars' worth of pennies?"

I looked at him. Thought of Ray Stevens.

I did not want to spend a hundred dollars on pennies.

"Yes," I said.

That day I went to the bank and bought 200 rolls of pennies. The teller handed them to me in a small canvas bag.

I took it to our safe deposit box. But our safe deposit box was about an inch high and 10 inches wide.

The bag was as big as a volleyball.

I walked out to my VW Squareback, opened the door, looked around inside.

The bag was too big for the glove compartment. Too inviting to leave on the back floor.

I thought for a moment.

Then I jammed the bag underneath the driver's seat.

At least now if the Russians do come over the border I'll have something to give them.

A hundred dollars was not peanuts to me so I tried to remember to lock the car.

Occasionally I'd check to be sure the bag wasn't visible to someone looking in.

But a few weeks later my security got lax.

I forgot about the 200 rolls of pennies under my seat.

Gradually the world's frenzy cooled off.

Gold, fear, imminent danger slipped from the news.

I slid back into my old ways.

I didn't lock the car.

Sometimes I even left the windows open.

Then one day, going through McDonald's, I was short of cash.

I remembered the pennies.

I reached around under the seat, felt my way into the bag and came out with four rolls…$2.

I tried not to lean on this source, but occasionally it was unavoidable.

Three dollars, six dollars, one dollar…but only as a last resort.

It had been months since the news mentioned the price of gold.

At 2 a.m. one morning I was driving over the Smoky Mountains.

Suddenly blue and white lights snapped on and blinked wildly in my mirror.

The Whoop! Whoop! of a siren raced up behind me.

I pulled over. We were up high. In the woods. It was cold.

The cop walked to my window, shined his flashlight into the back of the car, then on me.

"Eighty-one in a 65," he said. "What's the hurry?"

I stared out into the cold.

"Mind wandered, I guess, Officer…"

"Get your license and registration, bring them back to my car."

The bright dash lights in the cruiser glowed under the dome light as the officer wrote up my ticket.

It was warm in there. Better heater than my VW.

The trooper finished writing and tore off the page.

"Fifty-eight dollars," he said.

A hot flash shot through me.

"Now?" I said.

"Now. In this state over 80 is reckless driving. You pay or you stay."

"Stay?"

"In the tank."

"Until...?"

"You pay."

"I don't have $58."

"I can't help you there."

"Jail?" I thought, "Jesus."

"Pennies!!!" I said.

"Huh?"

"Will you take pennies?"

"Fifty-eight dollars' worth of pennies?"

"Maybe," I said, "can I see what I've got?"

The trooper looked at me.

"You think you've got fifty-eight bucks in pennies?"

"I might."

"Go for it," he said, "but try something funny and your ass is grass, you know that..."

"Yes."

With one hand resting on his holstered pistol, the trooper held his flashlight as I pulled my seat forward, reached underneath and came out with the canvas bag.

He shined his light into the bag.

He looked at me.

"This is bizarre as hell," he said.

"Put them in a pyramid in front of my headlights where I can count them."

One by one, I made rows of pennies until there were 116 rolls in a perfect pyramid on the roadside.

They sat up tall and looked neat in the glow of the headlights.

I was freezing. I could hear the cruiser's engine running.

With the toe of his boot, the trooper double-checked the count... shook his head in a slight shiver...and turned his face to me.

"All right," he said, "put them on my passenger seat."

I made another perfect pyramid on the seat of his car and we walked back out in front of his headlights.

I bent over and picked up the bag lying on the pavement.

"Anything left in there?" the trooper said.

I reached in and felt three rolls.

"Dollar fifty," I said.

That seemed to get his attention.

We stood looking at each other.

"You gonna be all right?" he said.

I smiled.

"Yes, I'm fine."

He took a few steps toward his car, then turned around.

"Hey," he said, "I gotta ask. Why all the pennies?"

I smiled.

"I bought them in case the Russians come over the Kentucky border."

He stared at me.

"Pennies?" he said.

"Copper."

For a few seconds he stood there and tapped his foot.

"Are the Russians coming over the border?"

"I don't know."

"But…" he said, waiting for the rest of the story.

"In case they do," I said.

He thought about that.

"If they do," he said, "I'd probably just shoot the bastards."

CHAPTER 19

When I got back in the driver's seat of my Volkswagen I noticed something.

I noticed I wasn't worried that this $58 speeding ticket would ruin my weekly budget, throw my life into havoc as it would have not long ago.

It hit me that I had gained some small measure of the freedom I'd first seen in action and craved years before when working for Benny Goodman: I was earning a living doing work I loved.

For a moment, on that dark highway in the middle of nowhere, I soaked-in the irony that as much as I had loved music all the years I worked for Benny, never once did it cross my mind that I might ever make a living in any form of the music business.

Benny's unspoken message to me was simply his lifestyle: work he loved, and a day he owned.

I remember how puzzled I was back then as to how to make such a life happen.

But now I was actually feeling a bit of this freedom, and I had a new perspective: *I do not have to make my life happen all by myself.*

Other people will help.

A lot of people had already helped me.

As a young person, I had no idea how much help I would need and would get along the way, and how much help we all need to get anywhere good in the world, or that every single solitary person who ever did get anywhere in the world could quickly recite a long list of those who had helped them get there.

As I started my car and eased back onto the Blue Ridge Parkway I thought of my own personal list.

For me, the lead helpers were my parents who raised me, and later Linda, to whom my parents handed me off and who has helped me the rest of the way.

But in among those three miraculous people, work and wanderlust had set me in touch with wise and kind men and women who, simply by being themselves, had tapped me into a steady river that has led to satisfaction and peace.

In that long and winding process a few things had become indelibly clear:

Nobody learns anything as well as they do when they try, fail, pay the consequences, and recover.

That simple cycle seems to be the one most-repeated by successful people.

I saw that the ability to simply keep going may be the most valuable of all skills.

I saw how much it helps to be able to state exactly what you want in one clear sentence, both to yourself and to anyone else, and then go for it.

I came to believe that it probably helps for kids to want something from life that their parents can't give them...so they have to go get it themselves.

I found that all of us human beings need respect almost more than we need food.

And I learned that sometimes a peppery comment from the right person can be a propellant of sorts.

I remembered our last day in Connecticut, when Linda and I stopped off at my parents' house with our VW bug loaded up for our move to Nashville and a hoped-for career as a songwriter, my dad had said, "Well, if all you want to be is a songwriter, I guess you're going to the right place."

That remark only hardened my resolve and must've played in my head a thousand times as I struggled to actually become a songwriter.

My Princeton-grad dad had boosted himself from a modest start to a terrific life, and one perfect for him.

He was an extremely responsible person, a great provider who opened doors to education and experiences that gave me confidence and that guide me every day.

Because of when my dad was born (1918), because of his simpler early circumstances and where he grew up (New Jersey), and because of his keen intelligence and his drive, my dad's most ready references and standards were related to pursuits and values associated more with traditional career paths than with the sensibilities I had.

Because of my great respect for him, a part of me wished that these leanings of his were mine, too.

But Nashville and its musical output were not a traditional career path. At least not where I came from.

Broke, but full of optimism and excitement, the moment Linda and I and our two young sons settled into our simple Nashville apartment I felt suddenly in the right place, suddenly at home.

Everywhere I went in Nashville I felt a "hug," a smile, and a good wish, even though no one knew me and status-wise I was below zero.

Part of that is because in Nashville, "wannabe songwriter" is not an unfamiliar job description.

Most every other would-be songwriter or singer had also come to town with nothing, loaded trucks, painted houses, tended bar, etc. to survive...and though that work ethic was no guarantee of success, people knew these basic jobs were how most songwriters kept afloat starting out...and that things could change quickly to the upside.

Before Kris Kristofferson's "Me And Bobby McGee," "Help Me Make It Through the Night," and other songs hit, Kris was a janitor at Columbia Records.

A few years later his child was in a private school and he shared a carpool with stockbrokers and doctors.

I met some of those stockbrokers and doctors and it helped to hear their tales. Instead of feeling behind and out of step as I had back in Connecticut, in Nashville I felt respected and wanted, even before one good thing had happened with my songs.

Some of this acceptance I felt from people was cultural. Nashville is an earthy, inclusive society.

And it is a society of storytelling and humor.

I love stories.

More often than not, even Nashville bankers and lawyers can tell you a memorable story.

Usually funny.

Because laughter works magic, brings people together, in Nashville I never once felt like an outsider.

The stories I heard touched me, educated me, and helped me get to know the people who told them.

Sonny Curtis, the brilliant songwriter, said that when he was a teenager a friend of his worked in a dry cleaners. Sometimes, to see what it might feel like to have money, he and his friend would go down to the cleaners after hours and try on other peoples' clothes.

(Did you feel a sudden tug on your heart? Me too.)

Banker John Stein described his mom's profound mood shift when she tiptoed at midnight into their family's den with an armload of Christmas presents and tripped over his sister and boyfriend having sex under the Christmas tree.

And I remember Hall of Fame songwriter and Mensa member Paul Craft giving me an insight into how a truly original member of our species thinks: Paul was tired of his current live-in girlfriend, Louise. Problem was he had lifted Louise from a modest lifestyle to one of nice clothes, Jaguars and Hawaiian trips. Now, he didn't feel he could just throw her out in the street. Every time I met Paul for coffee he was down in the dumps. "It's Louise," he said, "if I don't take care of her anymore, what'll happen to her?"

Then one day we met for coffee and Paul was all sunny smiles and happy.

"Paul," I said, "why the big change?"

He said, "I'm relieved about Louise."

I said, "Good, why?"

Paul said, "Because today on Craigslist I saw a beekeeping outfit for sale: beekeeping boots, beekeeping pants, belt, jacket, helmet, big beekeeping gloves...I thought WHO THE HELL IS GONNA WANT *THAT*?

"Then" Paul said, "a lightbulb went off: I realized somebody IS gonna want that stuff...and somebody's gonna want Louise, too."

Stories and turns of mind like Sonny's and John's and Paul's put me deeper and deeper in love with my new home and my new business.

Along with Nashville's cultural charm, better and better things happened with my songs.

Two summers after the "Rub It In" success, one of those angels we all need sat down beside me.

Bob Beckham was a famous music publisher in Nashville. He had published Kris Kristofferson's "Me and Bobby McGee" and "Help Me Make It Through The Night," Tony Joe White's "Rainy Night In Georgia" and "Polk Salad Annie," Billy Swan's "I Can Help" and Elvis' "Burnin' Love," among many others.

He was widely loved, respected, and a tireless worker. Out pitching my own songs, I would often run into Bob in the waiting rooms of record producers' offices, on the sidewalk as he high-stepped to appointments, or in one of Nashville's funky lunch spots.

Sometimes if there was a birthday at his company, he'd invite me to the party.

One day in someone's outer office we were seated side by side, each waiting our turn to play our songs...me the ones I'd written, Bob the ones written by writers he represented.

On this day, he turned to me with his characteristic smile…one that managed to convey both humor and dead-seriousness.

"You work your ass off," he said.

I was shocked and moved by the sudden compliment from the master songman.

"Thank you," I said.

"You got anything for Elvis?"

Elvis? Are you kidding? I must've mailed him 25 songs and gotten nowhere.

But Bob Beckham had a direct line to Elvis, through Felton Jarvis, Elvis' producer.

Everyone knew that Felton dropped by Bob's office every few weeks and picked up songs from his stable of incredible songwriters.

He had just asked me if I had any songs for Elvis.

"Yes," I said, "I do."

"Get them to my office by 3 o'clock. I'll give them to Felton."

"You will?"

"Damn right."

At the time, Elvis would only listen to specially cut lacquer discs. No cassettes. No tape.

Apparently he'd listen on a cheap record player right in the studio and sometimes if he didn't like what he heard he'd frisbee the disc right across the room.

Getting a lacquer disc cut was expensive.

I cleared the cost with Ray Stevens: I could put one song on each side of the disc.

Back in our tape room I listened to all the songs I thought were contenders. I narrowed it down to three. With the three in my hand, I had all but decided which two I'd send to Elvis.

As I got to the front door I told Ray's longtime assistant Shirley the three I was choosing from and asked which two she'd pick.

"I'd send 'Way Down'," she said.

It was the one I'd decided to eliminate.

But, I took Shirley's gut feeling as an omen and quickly revised my two choices.

I got the lacquers cut, took "Way Down" and the other song to Bob Beckham's office, and promptly forgot about it.

A week later, Ray Stevens came and found me in my broom closet office.

"Felton just called, he loves 'Way Down,' thinks Elvis will go crazy for it."

What?

I bolted for the car to race home and tell Linda.

Weeks passed. I heard nothing. Soon the incredible high I'd been on slipped away and the possibility that had seemed so real had all but disappeared.

Four months later, I heard a rumor on the street that Elvis was again looking for songs.

I took "Way Down" back to Bob Beckham's office.

Two days later I was in a windowless room at Decca Records phoning radio stations with a recording artist who'd recently released another one of my songs as a single. Our calls were an effort to get radio programmers to add the record to their playlists.

In between phoning the stations, the intercom rang for me.

"Bob Beckham's office is on line five for you."

I picked it up. It was Beckham's assistant, Carolyn.

"Layng," she said, "I think Elvis has already recorded this song."

Pause.

"Recorded it? Carolyn, I would know…."

"Well," she said, "let me check, call you right back."

My face got hot. I hung up the phone.

Three minutes later she called back.

"Yes," she said, "he recorded it on October 30th in the Jungle Room at Graceland."

I found it hard to believe my ears.

"God," I said, trying to grasp the moment, "that's totally incredible."

A week after that Felton Jarvis called Ray's office and asked for me.

"Layng," he said, "I'm mixing 'Way Down' at Creative Workshop...if you want to, come over and listen."

Mixing is the process, after all recording is done, when all the recorded tracks are finally mixed together, balanced...more bass drum, less rhythm guitar, etc....echo or reverb added, and so on.

I jumped in my primer-spotted Volkswagen that had no head-liner inside (yes, we now had a good house, but a slick car for me was low on my wishlist) and flew the three miles to the studio.

In the studio's dirt driveway was a van with a large western scene, including horses, painted in bright pastels on the side panels.

I got out of my car and stared.

There it was.

Felton's van.

Part of the Felton Jarvis legend.

I shook my head in a brief shiver of respect, and walked into the low white clapboard building that housed Creative Workshop.

My heart was racing.

No sooner had I stepped across the threshold than I heard a bass and drum pounding through the walls.

I stopped short.

Oh!

It was the introduction to "Way Down."

Suddenly an unmistakable voice began to sing.

Elvis Presley.

Singing my song.

For a moment I couldn't move a muscle.

"Jesus," I thought.

Then, tentatively…I pushed through the door to the control room.

The sound was so loud it rippled my clothes.

Whooosh!!! Brent Maher, the engineer, pushed the stop-button.

Silence.

I looked around.

No entourage. No crowd. Just me, Felton Jarvis, and Brent.

Jesus.

"Hey, Layng," Felton said, reaching out his hand and nodding toward the engineer, "you know Brent." We shook.

I'd never met either of them.

"Your song's a smash," Felton said, "got 'er just about mixed. Have a seat right here."

Felton tapped a spot on the couch, then turned his attention back to the mix.

"Hey, buddy," he said to Brent, "need a little more drums, we're selling excitement here."

"Got it," Brent said.

BOOM! The song came back on.

In the semi-darkness, I leaned back, closed my eyes and listened.

For a moment, I was back in my mom's station wagon with my seventh grade girlfriend, the radio is on, I'm hearing Elvis…and HEARTBREAK HOTEL…for the very first time…it's the night when I took my arm from around my girl, leaned forward toward the front seat and said, "Mom, please turn it up, who is that?"

Now, two decades later, I'm sitting on the couch in a Nashville recording studio with my eyes closed and Elvis is singing a song I wrote.

"How did this happen?" I wondered, almost out loud.

"Way Down" was released as a single in early June of 1977.

It took off quickly, but I held my breath every week when the new chart numbers came out, hoping the rise would continue.

On the 14th of August my family and I were in Rhode Island on vacation.

I was playing tennis when the tennis pro's assistant came to the edge of the grass.

"Layng," she said, "you have a phone call."

The tennis court was next to an old barn where the tennis pro had his office.

It was unusual to get a call there.

"Really?" I said.

"Yes. Someone from Nashville."

I leaned my racquet against the net and went inside to the phone. "Hello?"

"Hey, Layng, Frank Mull."

Frank was an independent record promotion man and a good friend. He was hired by music publishers, recording artists and sometimes by record companies to help get their records played on the radio. Music charts were the lifeblood of Frank's work, his report card...charts from radio stations in small cities, mid-size cities and big cities, all of them funneling into the national charts of *Billboard Magazine*.

Frank knew most everything that happened. Often, before it happened.

I hadn't hired Frank, so I knew this was not a business call.

"Hey, Frank, what's up?"

Suddenly, I realized what must be up...

"Just got the advance numbers from *Billboard*, buddy. 'Way Down' is #1 in next week's magazine."

As much as I'd been hoping for that, more than anything else the official word was a relief.

"That's totally incredible, Frank. Thank you."

"My pleasure," he said. "Go tie one on."

I put the phone back in its cradle.

"Good news?" said the tennis pro's assistant.

I smiled.

"Yes," I said, "very good."

I wasn't telling anyone until I'd told Linda.

Two days later I was on the same tennis court.

Again, a phone call.

This time, I had no idea what it could be.

"Hello?"

"Layng, it's Rose," said the voice in her New Orleans/Brooklyn accent. Rose Palermo, my Nashville attorney, the one who had handled our bankruptcy four years before.

"Rose, hey…"

"Are you near a television?"

"No."

"Elvis is dead."

"Way Down" was the last new song Elvis ever recorded.

I never met him.

I am certainly no more than a footnote in his career.

The sheet music from "Way Down" is in a frame on the wall of the library in our house.

It's now been 40 years since that single was released.

In many ways, that day seems like another lifetime.

There have been many "lifetimes" since.

Other dreams have come true.

Most days, I don't notice the sheet music hanging there with Elvis' picture on it and my name as the writer not far his name. But sometimes I do. And occasionally, I stop and stare.

I think of Bob Beckham getting "Way Down" to Elvis.

I think of the failures from which I wondered if I'd ever recover.

I think of the years that Linda did without, of the trucks I loaded, the faith that Linda, my mom, and Ray Stevens kept burning so brightly inside me and of the sheer luck that so often steers our lives.

I think of our three strong boys, grown now and making their own good ways in the world and I think of Linda asleep upstairs.

I think how empty my life would be without those four people.

And as much as I know you can't always get what you dream of…

232 —   LAYNG MARTINE JR.

I know that sometimes you get even more.

Elvis' record of "Way Down" was a confirmation of sorts, affirmation that I had found my "thing," that I had found a way of earning a living that I loved. And songwriting offered the freedom of time and spirit I had always dreamed of. I never missed one of our boys' teachers' conferences, a school play or a baseball game. And every single morning when I woke up I was free to make up my day any way I wanted.

As long, of course, as the hits kept coming.

While "Way Down" was the beginning of a new level of excitement and satisfaction for me in my work, as well as a source of new energy for the future, it was also an ending of sorts.

To me, and many others, Elvis was the most idolized, revered recording artist who ever lived.

The idea that he had recorded a song of mine and been successful with it seemed impossible.

But it had happened.

That event gave me a feeling I couldn't have bought with all the money in the world, and a feeling I could not possibly have anticipated.

I was 35.

Even with so many years to live, and so much work still to do, I felt a period at the end of some unspoken sentence.

A bow on some beautiful package that I never knew existed.

And for a brief moment I stopped and drank it in.

CHAPTER 20

Three years after Elvis' death, in the winter of 1980, I began to crave recordings by certain singers not living in or making their records in Nashville. And, though I was sending songs to New York and LA producers, I got no response from them and began to get frustrated.

I had two thoughts on what to do about that, how to have a shot at records made in other music centers.

One thought was to join forces with Bob Beckham, the publisher who had so generously given "Way Down" to Elvis' producer, Felton Jarvis.

Bob had had so much music publishing success over many years and knew people everywhere, having begun his own career as a song-writer and singer, including his start as Brenda Lee's opening act in the early 60s.

My other idea was to sign with Irwin Schuster at Chappell Music in New York.

In the 17 years since I'd played my first song, "Swagger," for Irwin in between my Columbia University classes, he had become the most celebrated pop music publisher in the U.S.

Irwin was now the creative head of Chappell, a giant worldwide music publisher, with access to everyone who made records and needed songs.

We had bumped into each other over the years at awards dinners and music gatherings and a great respect and affection had grown between us. I was already good friends with Henry Hurt who ran Chappell's Nashville office.

After some sleepless nights, I decided on Chappell.

We agreed to a three-year partnership.

On one of the most emotional days of my life I told Ray Stevens that I would be leaving his company.

I explained that I had to try for some records by artists I loved who were based elsewhere and who I'd been unable to get through to via mail and phone calls and that I hoped Chappell could get me records by some of these people.

Ray and I were sitting in his office.

He tapped his fingers on his desk when I finished my few sentences and a brotherly smile broke on his face.

"I knew this day would come, Layng," he said. "We've had a hell of a run."

A few days later I handed Ray my set of keys to his building.

I went out to my car and cried in the parking lot.

One of the enduring and happiest aspects of the 37 years since that day is the great expressed affection and respect Ray and I have continued to have for each other.

We meet for lunches, and we talk about everything that matters.

At the start of most every year, I make a fresh attempt, in writing, to thank Ray for his teaching, his early financial backing, for his faith in me from the moment we met and from the moment we moved our young family to Nashville.

I usually spend quite a bit of time writing this "thank you" letter.

But it always feels inadequate.

Without Ray's help, it's likely I would've had to do something else to provide for my family and therefore been unable to pursue music with the focus and intensity required to be successful.

The first three songs I wrote after leaving Ray and under my new agreement with Chappell led to more sleepless nights and second-thoughts about my decision to sign with Chappell over Bob Beckham.

These first three songs I turned in to Chappell were all more oriented toward pop music than country music and therefore would be listened to and evaluated up in New York by Irwin Schuster. As much as I loved and admired Irwin, sending my songs off to him in New York was so different from knocking on Ray's door with a new song and asking to play it for him and getting feedback immediately. I worried that I needed someone with whom I could be with face-to-face daily, playing my new songs and pooling thoughts on what recording artists might like to record them.

That worry made me think I should have signed with Bob Beckham, who was right here in Nashville and available every day.

So, two days after turning in my first three songs, I walked into Chappell's Nashville office to ask-out of my newly-inked deal.

When I walked into the office of Chappell's Nashville boss Henry Hurt, Henry lit up.

"Layng," he said, "I just got off the phone with Irwin. He says that new song you sent him 'Should I Do It?' is the best new song he's received in years and he's sure he'll get you a great record on it!"

Suddenly my resolve to quit Chappell disappeared.

I became eaten up with the possibilities Irwin believed he could deliver and began to write new songs in a fury.

Quickly, Chappell got "Should I Do It?" recorded by The Pointer Sisters, great pop stars of that time, and the song became a top 10 pop hit.

I was so excited and encouraged I could barely stand it.

A daily routine took shape.

Most every morning, I would call Irwin and we would discuss what artists were looking for songs and which of mine might suit them. On days when he had just listened to one of my new songs he'd give me his feedback, which could be anything from, "Not sure this one's doing it for me," to "I love it, gonna play it for Clive Davis (the fabled music executive) this afternoon," to "This may be more of a movie song than a hit single. Let me see what I can come up with."

When a second song was recorded by The Pointer Sisters and became the B-Side of a 45 RPM single instead of the A-Side, which is the side promoted to the radio stations, I got a copy of the 45, raced home and played it.

I loved the Pointers' recording of the song and FedExed it overnight to Irwin in New York.

Irwin loved the version, too, and played it for Clive Davis who was looking for songs for Barry Manilow.

Clive loved the song but wanted me to write a third section, a "bridge" after the second chorus that would lead back into a final reprise of the chorus.

I went to our kitchen table with my guitar and began working.

That night I wrote a bridge I liked, but decided to sleep on it and be sure I still loved it in the morning.

Next morning, I did still love it.

My cassette player was down at my office in town, so I went up to our son Tucker's room and used his.

I played the four new lines into Tucker's cassette player and as soon as I got a take I liked I FedExed the cassette to Irwin.

He played the cassette for Clive who loved it, and a few weeks later the song was recorded by Barry Manilow.

While not a single in the U.S., it was a single in many other countries, top 10 in the UK and on gold albums both there and in the United States.

With good things rolling on the music front we went for our summer week in Watch Hill, Rhode Island, the harborside village

I'd sailed into years ago on the *YOU'LL DO* with the Luders family, and where Linda's parents had bought a place soon after our wedding.

But that summer, there was a new tone to the visit.

Suddenly, with all the grandchildren and family members even this big old summer house with its many bedrooms now felt crowded and noisy, no longer the peaceful haven it had always been.

We wished we could afford a Watch Hill place of our own.

But houses there were way beyond our budget.

Then one day, walking along the Watch Hill harbor an idea lit up.

"What we should own," I said, "is one of these buildings along the harbor. We could live on the second floor, have a view of the water, and get help paying for it from renting out the shops below."

Linda loved the idea and it became our obsession.

This was before realtors had the Multiple Listing Service, or MLS, so most brokers kept their listings in simple three-ring notebooks, or in their pockets.

At 10 a.m. the next morning a broker friend and I sat in a booth inside Watch Hill's elegant old village restaurant.

Opening the broker's small notebook, I leafed past the homes for sale to the commercial properties listed in the back.

There weren't many.

Suddenly I turned the page and saw a building I knew well.

I looked at the rents.

I looked at the price.

In order to stay afloat the past 10 years I'd bought and sold quite a few houses so I saw immediately that the price and the rents of the building were out of whack, in my favor.

But most of all, I knew that the location of this building was incomparable.

It overlooked the village green and out directly over Watch Hill Harbor, filled all summer long with sailboats and activity.

I couldn't imagine that anyone would ever want to sell that building.

"Can we go in it right now?" I said. "If these rents are accurate we'll buy it today."

Twenty minutes later I'd rounded up Linda and she and I and the broker stepped out onto the third floor porch of the building where Linda and I made no attempt to hide our personal versions of a gasp. The view from the porch was of three states: Rhode Island, and out across the water, Connecticut, and Fishers Island, New York.

For some reason, no real estate contracts were on hand so, since I had typed up quite a few such agreements over the past few years, I typed out the basic terms, signed it and handed it to the broker.

"Are you sure you don't want to make an offer first?" the broker said. "The building's been on the market two years without any interest."

"No," I said.

We bought the building that day for the asking price.

I knew this building would change our lives forever and it was already a steal, why waste one second and give an errant piece of bad luck a chance to slip in?

I was so spooked and emotionally invested in getting this building that in the two months before closing I left my wristwatch on Rhode Island time during the whole nail-biting eight weeks back in Nashville, where time runs one hour earlier.

In my imagination, I pictured the following summer. When school let out, the five of us would drive to Watch Hill and…while the kids played tennis and went to the beach…Linda and I would scrape, spackle and paint every room in our upstairs apartment and eat our lunch every day overlooking what we thought the most beautiful view in the world.

And that's what we did.

It was the first of our 33 summers in those wonderful, sunny rooms.

In 2007 when the stock market and lots of wallets were inflated, someone offered us an immense amount of money for the building. Enough money for any three families to live nicely for the rest of their lives. We said no. Even when they came back a second time, we didn't consider selling. Even for a moment. It's not that we wouldn't have loved that cash in our account, but sitting on our deck together with our coffee or a glass of wine is better than money.

In 1984, at the end of our first Watch Hill summer as home-owners, Irwin and I were going on four years together, during which time he and his company got me more of the recordings I'd previously only dreamed about, including the theme ("Believe In The Beat,") to a kids' dance movie, earning me special kudos from our boys.

Irwin's boundless access and can-do nature was the most powerful drive-factor I could imagine because I believed if I wrote something really good, he could and would get it to the right people.

Day and night and on weekends, I wrote songs. Seeing and hearing me play my guitar and sing in the kitchen or wherever was a most common sight for our three boys.

Because I'd grown up with four younger brothers and sisters where raised voices and chaos was the norm, I could write songs amid most any drama and excitement going on around me. And, since I loved being wherever Linda and the boys were, mid-chaos was often where I was found making my own form of noise.

Around our house, the name "Irwin" had come to mean "He Who Can Work Magic" to Linda and me and our older two sons.

If I ever came home and Linda said, "Irwin just called, he said to call him, he's got good news for you," my heartbeat would rocket up and I'd race to the phone.

Rarely was there ever "good news" like the "good news" delivered by Irwin.

Then one morning I called him. First thing, as always.

His secretary said he'd not yet arrived.

I called back later.

But Irwin never did come in that day.

Or the next.

On the third morning when his secretary said he'd not arrived, I said, "Lori, this is impossible.

Irwin has never even been late for work let alone missed a day. What's going on?"

She burst into tears.

"Layng," she said, "Irwin is dead."

Silence.

I fell apart.

"How?" I said in sobs.

She didn't answer.

"How, Lori?" I said, louder.

"He jumped off the balcony of his apartment," she said.

I heard that Irwin left a note, but I never saw it. I never spoke with anyone who did.

And the "Why? "…as much as I ached to know…was none of my business.

All that mattered was that a golden man, and a golden moment, were gone.

The years following Irwin's death were fallow for me. Even before he died I'd lost a little passion and, though I still wrote every day, I'd already written so many songs that now I often wondered what more I cared to write about.

I rarely felt moved or inspired by anything I heard from my voice or my guitar.

Before Irwin's death, I'd had him to talk with about this change.

He said such periods were normal, and I think I was slowly climbing out of it.

Irwin had become like a dad, or a big brother…someone always there with whom I could talk about anything.

Now with Irwin gone, it was lonesome. Every day.

I went to my office, but rarely wrote. What I did write didn't sound very good, even to me.

I would go to the library a lot of days and just read newspapers or magazines, by the fire in winter, otherwise at the large common table. Two years after Irwin's leap from his balcony, Chappell chose not to renew my contract, and I didn't blame them…neither of us thought much of the songs I'd written.

I'd go to my office, go to lunch with friends, occasionally play tennis, go for walks…I was nowhere near being in the music business with my heart, mind and both feet the way I had been for so long. Of course, along with my malaise came no new recordings of my songs which made me feel even more out of it.

One day Shirley called me from Ray Stevens' office to say that S.C. Johnson, the makers of Pledge, Windex, Drano, Off!, Saran Wrap, etc., had a new product called Glade Plug-Ins and wanted to use "Rub It In" in several test markets, changing the chorus from "Rub it in…" to "Plug it in…" The combination of product and song tested through the roof and S.C. Johnson went national with Glade Plug-Ins in a massive TV campaign.

Glade Plug-Ins and the TV commercials were an immediate success.

Friends all over the country were hearing it and people who had been in our backyard the day the simple song was written were in shock.

So was I.

The commercials ran for 18 years.

That brought in money, for which I was very grateful. But I still felt unproductive and lost.

Six years after Irwin's death when I'd strum my guitar strings

I felt as though I'd heard that sound a million times before, and it didn't do a thing for me.

The great excitement that had brought forth my hit songs was missing and I didn't know how to get it back.

I had loved writing my songs alone and prided myself on being able to write words and music that great and famous singers wanted to sing. But now I needed help, some new thoughts, new sounds, and a fresh way of looking at songwriting. And I realized I could also use a buddy to look at across the table in the morning instead of looking at an empty room and blank page.

Toward the end of that period I wrote one of the few songs about unhappiness I've ever written called "Can't Hide Away." Recently I pulled out the simple guitar/vocal version I'd made 26 years ago on my cassette recorder the day I wrote the song. Just listening to the voice for 15 seconds I can hear the ache and the pain in the sad person who's singing: me.

I decided to call some of the best songwriters I knew to see if they would consider writing with me.

Those calls were hard to make because I didn't know what would happen, if anyone would say yes.

I was thrilled to find that some did.

The day I went to my first co-writing session I had a talk with myself.

"Layng," I said, "be sure to shut up today. You called this guy because he's written huge hits by himself, so when he has an opinion about the words, the music, the concept, whatever…listen."

This talk was necessary because when you write alone you don't have to listen to anybody, get anybody's "yes" vote on a word or line or melody or idea. But the whole reason I was going to this appointment was to get another person's ideas, his words, his approach, his suggestions. I was sick of just hearing mine.

Grammy-winning songwriter Richard Leigh ("Don't It Make My Brown Eyes Blue") had just bought a new house and so far the only furniture in it was a card table and a few folding chairs. As rooms-to-write-in go, that sparse space was perfection to my eyes. And right in front of the card table was a gas log fireplace that we lit to stave off the February chill.

We slid two of the folding chairs near each other and sat down a few feet apart holding our guitars.

"Got any ideas you're crazy about?" I said.

Richard broke out laughing.

"That's funny," he said.

Then he struck a few strings on his ancient Martin guitar and said, "I've got this title I think could be something…"

"What is it?"

"'The Greatest Man I Never Knew'," he said.

The minute Richard said that I remembered that his dad had died before Richard was old enough to know him.

Now I smiled.

"Well," I said, "the greatest man I never knew lived right down the hall from me."

Richard's eyes got wide, he stared at me for a few seconds, "WOW!" he said, "we're rolling!"

It took Richard and me five consecutive days to write that song.

It's a song about a non-communicative father.

Sometimes the lines we suggested to each other made us laugh so hard we nearly choked to death. And sometimes the lines were so true and painful that it was all we could do not to stop writing for the day and let the ache wear off and our thoughts clear.

I recently found the original lyrics to "The Greatest Man I Never Knew," words written on a yellow pad from the very first day we began working, including some lines and verses that took us off in what now looks like a horribly wrong direction and which, by some miracle, we didn't follow.

Richard sang the demo, and as much as we loved the song and as much as it moved people to tears, some very smart and successful music people shied away from recording it because the song was so heartbreaking. One huge star said he thought it would be a massive hit but that he couldn't record it because listeners would think it represented his own relationship with his dad, which it didn't.

Then, a friend got the song to Reba McEntire.

Reba's single of the song reached #1. But when she first heard the last verse, in which the dad dies without ever saying he loved her, Reba's first instinct was that the dad shouldn't die. It was too sad.

Producer Tony Brown called Richard and told him Reba would like the line changed. I was out of town and didn't know about Tony's call, but Richard explained to Tony that the power of the song was that the dad was gone, that there was no chance for him to go back and make up for what he had not done…say he loved his daughter.

Tony saw Richard's point, explained our position to Reba, she understood, and agreed that the song as written was right.

Apart from Reba's single reaching #1, the initial album containing "The Greatest Man I Never Knew" sold five million copies.

The song also appeared on two of Reba's later CDs, selling an additional seven million copies.

It had been a while since I'd had a hit and it felt very good to have one, especially one that resonated with so many people.

And it also felt good to finally have a payday again.

It was about this time that I wrote a song called "Life Is A Wild Place."

Here are the song's first verse and chorus:

Nothing seems so certain anymore
Once you realize there are no rules
How to survive may be the only thing worth knowing
And they don't teach us that in school

Life is a wild place
You got to be ready for love, ready for war
Ready for less and a little bit more
Open your heart and lock your door
A lion may purr and a kitten may roar
Life is a wild place

As I wrote this song I had no idea how wild our life was about to get.

CHAPTER 21

That June, as had become our tradition, Linda and I set out for Watch Hill with our youngest son, Mac, 15.

So that we could have two cars in Rhode Island, Linda and Mac drove in her station wagon and I followed in my longtime favorite, a red 1966 Mustang convertible.

Our two cars stayed together on I-40 for three hours.

Then, something went wrong with mine.

We stopped in Knoxville at a repair shop.

The fix was going to take a while.

No sense in Linda and Mac waiting around.

Linda was wearing a blue and white seersucker dress as she and Mac walked to her car. It was the last time I would ever see her walk. As they pulled away, she called out, "See you in a few hours!" and blew a kiss.

I blew one back.

We planned to meet up later at a motel in Allentown, Pennsylvania.

Have you ever come upon a traffic jam on the Interstate and looked for an exit to try your luck on the back roads?

It was late. I was impatient. Traffic was stopped in both directions.

Finally I managed to move to the shoulder and scoot along to an exit, where I found an empty frontage road running parallel to the highway. Barely onto it, I saw a cluster of blinking blue lights in the distance.

Wow, what happened?

Without knowing it, I had driven within 200 feet of my family.

I wondered if Linda and Mac were already at the motel, or if they were also stuck in this jam.

Then I thought: Could they be in that accident? But wait — of course not. They were way ahead.

A while later I stopped at a diner, where I found a pay phone and dialed the motel. When I asked for the Martine room, the desk clerk said, "There's someone on the other line calling for Martine, too."

"Who?"

"Someone from the hospital in Hershey."

"Can you connect me?"

"No, but they gave me their number."

I hung up and redialed, my face hot. The woman who answered identified herself as the hospital chaplain. She said my family had been in an accident.

"Are they all right?"

She put the doctor on, who told me that my son was O.K. My wife, however, was a different story.

I listened as he described her condition, then asked, "Can she think?"

"Yes. Her brain is fine."

And that's when I knew we could do it, long before I had any idea what "it" was.

Three months of surgeries, rehab, individual classes, lessons, and weekly lectures followed before we began to find out.

We were on our way home to Nashville and it was our first night away from the skill and comfort of the nurses we had come to depend on.

From our room at the Roanoke, VA Marriott, we ordered wine and a beautiful dinner delivered to us by room service.

We ate together by candlelight.

We toasted each other many times, excited to be out of the hospital, grateful to be together and heading home.

That night we fell asleep wrapped in each other's arms for the first time in months.

So far, so good.

Then we woke up and smelled something. It smelled like a bowel movement. I lifted up the sheets.

It was a bowel movement, and it was in our bed.

We knew we had a lot to learn, but we had no idea how much.

Hearing the word paraplegic had made us focus on the big thing, the fact that Linda could no longer walk. Less anticipated were the smaller humiliations and inconveniences, like bowel movements in bed or on the way to a party, sores that came out of nowhere and took months or years to heal, and inaccessible restroom stalls that caused Linda to have to catheterize herself in the public area where people were washing their hands and talking.

And on it went, the list of indignities. She couldn't watch "Good Morning America" if the remote fell off the bed when she reached for her glasses. She wet the seat on airplanes and in friends' cars. She could no longer feel sexual intercourse (and the powerful muscle spasms in her legs threatened to crush anyone who tried).

But we've learned, and adapted. Now we know the places with good handicapped-access bathrooms (Starbucks), which airline makes things easiest (Southwest), which cities have smooth curb cuts (San Francisco), and which movie theaters don't make us sit four feet from the screen.

Anyone who is in love is living a charmed life, especially if you've been in love for many years, through good times and bad. I have been crazy about Linda since the first time I saw her. We always felt we could handle any challenge because we were facing it together. This time we knew we had the will, but the demands were so exhausting, the changes so pervasive, that sometimes we wondered how we would cope.

This incredibly capable woman who loved to hike mountains, ride waves, and run marathons, who had cleared our sizable backyard of eight-foot-high brambles and helped me move all our furniture into three houses, suddenly couldn't do any of those things, ever again.

Not long after getting home from the hospital, when we were having dinner by candlelight at our kitchen table, she burst into tears. "I don't know if I can do this for the rest of my life," she said.

All I could say was, "We'll do it together."

We began to think of what we could do to replace playing tennis, walking on the beach, working in the garden. Since Linda loves the ocean, a friend found a specially designed beach chair made of PVC tubing with wide inflated tires that allow it to be pushed across the sand. It's yellow and white with a big red umbrella.

The first time I saw Linda sitting atop those tubes and under the red umbrella, I told her she looked like Ronald McDonald's home-coming queen.

She laughed like crazy, then repeated it to everyone she knew.

A few summers later, one of our three sons suggested that he and I get on either side of the chair, slide Linda off, carry her into the ocean and drop her just beyond the waves so she could float calmly behind the crashing breakers.

At first we put her in a life preserver, but she tipped over and couldn't right herself. So we took it off, and to our surprise she bobbed peacefully, looking once again like every other person lolling in the sea on a summer day.

You know those great old stores on Newbury Street in Boston with five or six steps up to each one? At first we could get up only about three of those a day. Now we can do every single store, one right after the other, all day long. My arms and my back are stronger

— so are Linda's — and there's a rhythm to our teamwork that's become second nature to us.

We take many more drives now, preferably in our convertible, looking for pretty roads and funky hamburger places, especially '50s-style drive-ins where they bring the food to our car. Before the car even moves an inch, though, Linda has to put on her seat belt, because even a semi-sudden stop at low speed will whap her face against the dashboard as if she's a spring-loaded bobblehead.

She has no stomach muscles. Her body works only from the chest up.

I remember the day we had to tell her that. She was in the ICU, tubes all over, machines and screens whirring and blinking, traces of dried blood in her gnarled hair. The doctor and I stood on either side of her bed.

"Linda," he said, "this accident you were in was a rough one."

"I can tell," she said, her words warped by the breathing tube.

"At the moment your legs do not move."

She looked at him. "Will they?"

"I doubt it."

Her eyes shifted over to me. I squeezed her hand gently.

After the doctor left, tears filled her eyes. "It was all too perfect," she said, "wasn't it?"

And it did seem that way.

It always had, since the moment I saw her through the screen door of her Georgia house.

Soon it will be 25 years since Linda's accident.

What we've learned has made all the difference.

We know that most people — strangers, anywhere — will knock themselves out to help us if we explain what we need. We know to say "Yes" to nearly everything because there is probably a way to do it. We know there is happiness available every day, most of it requiring more effort than money. And effort seems like a small price to pay for a day at the beach, a trip to New York or for dinner up eight steps to a friend's home.

A few months after the accident, Linda started driving again. Her car has hand controls. She thinks nothing of driving to visit her father two hours away by herself. She has rolled three marathons — yes, a full 26-plus miles in a racing wheelchair.

And now, so long since that fateful night, looking at Linda across the dinner table, or seeing her across the room at a party, the hopeless crush I have on her is as wonderfully out of control as when I first saw her more than five decades ago through the screen door. I still get excited after work when I pull in the driveway and know that I'll soon get to see the sexy, beautiful, very funny person I live with. And, later on, snuggle up to her in bed.

We've rolled up and down the hills of Tuscany, squeezed into pubs in Ireland, explored narrow streets in Paris and Rome, gone to Red Sox games, had coffee in the sunshine in San Francisco, Portland, Chicago and Miami. And we've learned that alongside great loss we can still have a great life. We want it so badly, and we love it so much.

During Linda's months in the Pennsylvania hospital I had come home to Nashville only once.

The main purpose of my trip was to figure out how to ready our house for comfortable living by a person in a wheelchair.

An elevator was the most major change necessary, and exactly where that should go was obvious right away. In addition, we needed two ramps...one at the front door, and one down nine inches to the living room floor and the elevator.

Once getting those changes in motion I went to my secondary purpose: making a demo of a new song I loved called "I Was Blown Away."

The musicians laid down a wonderful musical track of the song and Reba McEntire's sometime-duet-partner, the brilliant Linda Davis, sang the vocal.

The result was a sensational demo.

"I Was Blown Away" was recorded by the reigning CMA Female Vocalist of the Year, Pam Tillis.

This recording was particularly meaningful to me for two reasons.

First, I had written it by myself and, at 53, was edging toward the older side to be writing hit singles alone. I was thrilled it had happened.

But, there was another reason. Most of the money earned from "The Greatest Man I Never Knew" had gone for expenses related to Linda's car accident: elevators in both our Nashville and Rhode Island houses, various ramps, and an extensive remodel/reshaping of the Rhode Island house.

The prospect of a fresh cash infusion was most welcome.

Apart from being named CMA Female Vocalist of the Year, Pam Tillis had just had two #1 records in a row.

Now, mine was teed up to be the third.

At that moment in Nashville, there was no more coveted single to have than one by Pam Tillis.

Pam's single of "I Was Blown Away" was released and racing up the charts when the Murrah Building in Oklahoma City blew up and 168 people were "blown away" in the blast.

When I heard about the explosion on the news the morning it happened I made no association between that event and my record.

But that night, we were out at dinner with friends when the conversation turned to the subject of "life imitating art" and "art imitating life."

Suddenly, in horrific clarity, I saw the connection between the day's devastating explosion in Oklahoma and the title of my new record.

All day long on every TV network I had watched a parade of reporters standing in front of the gnarled ruins of the Murrah Building saying, "Here today 168 people were blown away" over and over and over.

Now, sitting there at a round dinner table with five dear friends, I knew beyond a shadow of doubt that my record was over.

I said nothing.

My head spinning, I did my best to go on with the convivial gathering.

But my mind was not there.

When we got outside after dinner, it was raining as I wheeled Linda to our car. Helping her into the front seat I could contain my emotions no longer.

I stopped a moment, looked at her, and said, "My record is over."

Rain pelting my face, I folded the wheelchair and put it in the trunk of our car.

Then I slipped in behind the wheel and stared at the raindrops splattering like liquid bullets against the windshield.

"Amazing," I said, "gone. The Oklahoma bombing today..."

Linda looked over, puzzled.

"What does that bombing have to do with your record?" she said.

"Unfortunately," I said, "everything."

When we walked in the door of our house I went to our answering machine and punched "messages."

"Layng," said the first voice, "this is Mike Robertson, Pam Tillis' manager, please call me when you get home, regardless of time."

Mike delivered the news I had dreaded.

"Layng," he said, "I have something very rough to tell you. Because of today's tragedy in Oklahoma City, radio stations everywhere are besieged with calls asking how they can play a song called 'I Was Blown Away' when 168 people actually were blown away today. As unrelated as these two things are, we have no choice but to pull the record. We will fax all radio stations we can reach who may be playing the song and ask them to please take the record off the air immediately out of respect for those killed and for their families."

A few nights later at our dinner table, I started to cry.

With Linda's accident, we had lost so much, and now I felt as though my business was slipping out from under me.

The one slash of humor generated by this situation was a flash of something my mom might have said under the circumstances, and that is, "It's not your fault, but it is your problem."

My smile was muted, to say the least.

For a long time, I couldn't talk about that record and what had happened.

It just hurt too much.

I kept writing.

Every day I carried my guitar and my red backpack full of lyrics and pens into a room where that day's co-writer and I would talk, laugh, and work.

Usually, that combination added up to a new song, or a good start on one.

Before I felt myself changing and leaning in altogether new directions, my dear friend Kent Robbins and I wrote "I Wanna Go Too Far" for Trisha Yearwood.

Trisha is such a fabulous singer and hearing her record of our song was a gigantic upper.

Years ago, fabled songwriter Bouldleaux Bryant ("Wake Up Little Susie," "All I Have To Do Is Dream") told me that songwriting is "a young man's game."

At the time he said that, I didn't really grasp what he meant.

But, getting older now, I understood.

Sure enough, what I cared about had begun to change.

Though I still loved my songs, and though sometimes late at night when Linda was asleep, I would put on earphones and scroll through the hundreds of songs I've written since 1963 and fall in love with some of them all over again, I gradually stopped waking up mornings with the urgency to write them as I had for so many years. Urgency like walking the Hartford, CT streets at 2 a.m. on our wedding night rifling through words and phrases in my head to complete a lyric. Or getting up pre-dawn to sit at a Waffle House counter shuffling through my cache of song titles, adding a few to the list in hopes of landing on a gem of an idea to write then and there.

During this time of change, in 2013, I was elected to the Nashville Songwriters Hall of Fame. To be linked in any way with the Hall's brilliant writers, including boyhood heroes like Johnny Cash and Chuck Berry, is an honor I did not expect. It shocked me. And thrilled me. Now I think about that honor a few times every day. I'm not sure exactly why I do. But I do.

The induction dinner was a warm celebration, with Linda, me, our boys, my brother Fang, Linda's brother Lee and his wife, and Ray Stevens all at the same table.

The honor was especially welcome because it came at the time when that fire I'd once had to write songs had cooled.

As is probably true in most things, to be successful as a songwriter, you have to be obsessed with it.

There is no such thing as a "gentlemen songwriter," someone who earns a good living year in and year out writing hit songs in his/her spare time.

At least, I've never met or heard of that person.

Instead, the need to write songs eats you up, chases you most hours of the day, impolitely whispering thoughts and ideas in your ear when you're involved in other things.

It's love. It's involuntary, and you can't stop it.

If someone is hopelessly in love with writing songs, "in it with both feet," it's no guarantee of success, but he or she at least has a chance.

More and more, what I was "in with both feet" were things involving Linda and our boys, and friends.

For a friendship, nothing is more magical than new adventures together in new places accompanied by dinners, a few glasses of wine, and no timetable.

My brother Fang and I take four quick trips a year, one in every season...two-night blowouts together talking about our parents, our siblings, the past, the present, and cruising country roads for pancakes, cheeseburgers, and ice cream in our stomping grounds: villages in all six New England states plus Montreal and Quebec.

When we walk into a restaurant Fang knows where I want to sit, and I know where he wants to sit. His choice: a quiet corner. My choice: in the middle of everything. Such differences provide every trip with enormous laughs...and easy compromise, because to be together we'll both sit anywhere.

One of our sons lives in Nashville. Linda and I usually see him multiple times weekly for coffee, lunch, or dinner. Our two other boys live in Portland, Oregon with their families...each has two boys. We go out there for several weeks or a month each year, they each come to Nashville once, and they visit us in Rhode Island every summer plus we get together in Nashville or Portland for Christmas.

I had an especially dear high school friend who lived in Colorado. He got cancer. His doctors said he would last a year or two.

From the time he got that news until the day he died 15 years later, he and I met most every quarter, usually in Chicago.

So, 50-plus get-togethers.

We'd have drinks and dinner, talk, and walk whatever city we were in, and we always included one "cultural event."

In Chicago we went to The Oprah Winfrey Show, the Commodities Exchange, the Museum of Surgery, Lincoln Park Zoo, the Broadcast Museum, many times to the Chicago Art Institute, multiple blues clubs and so on. Once we met in Nevada to tour the Hoover Dam, once in Newport, RI, to tour the mansions. We met in New Orleans and New York.

After one night and two days of conversation, meals and adventures, we'd get back on a plane and head home. Greatly enriched.

For seven years, another friend and I, both lovers of Paris, went to Paris for the weekend once a year on the same weekend Linda went to Chicago with three buddies. Our Paris mission was to eat eclairs, walk neighborhoods, have dinners, rarely sleep, and generally culture-up for 48 hours.

A college pal who at 18 said he wanted to be "a tycoon" and then became one, called up a few years ago to say he'd bought a 113-foot yacht in Europe and asked if Linda and I would like to come over and cruise the French Riviera for a while.

When I got up early our first morning onboard, we were moored far out in the middle of San Tropez Harbor.

Quietly I got dressed, slipped out of our stateroom, into the hall, outside along the gangway and up to the polished mahogany top deck.

I stopped.

I looked.

In the early morning light it seemed hundreds of yachts and sail-boats lay at anchor in calm silence all around us.

Not a sound.

Not a soul in sight.

But there, as if by magic, on a linen-and-silver-set breakfast table, lay today's *Wall Street Journal*, *USA Today* and the *International Herald Tribune* next to a crystal pitcher of fresh orange juice.

I sat down and wondered how I ever got to have such a beautiful seat, in such a beautiful place.

My first thought on that subject was simple: pure luck.

My second thought was how grateful I am to have had a mom who believed in life's glorious possibilities and who set me and my curiosity free so young.

As our boys got older, Linda and I got an idea we thought might help feed their own curiosity and dreams. We decided to offer them one round-trip plane ticket each year to any place in the world they wanted to go. But the corollary to that offer was that they had to earn all the rest of the money their trips required: food, lodging, train tickets, car rentals, etc. This relatively modest investment on our part paid huge dividends as the boys took advantage of it. Those plane tickets led to adventures in Africa, Greece, New Zealand, Spain,

Turkey, France, Morocco, Ireland, Italy, England and other countries. Most often the boys traveled alone, adding to the challenge of the trip and to their sense of accomplishment, and their confidence.

Not long ago at dinner in our Nashville kitchen, Linda and I talked about the lasting value of those solo adventures, the comfort the boys now have in unfamiliar situations, their willingness to take chances, and the excitement they feel for the huge world out there and for new people.

In the candlelight we clinked our glasses in a toast to my mom, who knew how much was to be gained by letting go.

CHAPTER 22

For me, now in my sixties, it wasn't long before a different kind of letting go took place.

I finally let go completely of my 40+ year obsession with song-writing and a new form of writing moved in.

I felt a wonderful replenishing of my creative energy as lots of the brainspace formerly occupied 24/7 by my quest for the irresistible song title now filled up with a new obsession: trying to put into words what Linda's and my life had been like in the years since her car accident.

It took me several years of writing…off and on…to finally get that story in a form I felt happy with.

When finished, I thought it might suit the readers of *O, The Oprah Magazine,* but, though their editor was encouraging, they did not accept my story.

Then, one Sunday after reading the "Modern Love" column in *The New York Times,* at the bottom I noticed an email address for submissions.

I stared at that opportunity for a moment before I said, "That's what our story is, modern love."

Thirty seconds later I clicked "send" and fired my work off into cyberspace.

The next afternoon I was in a Nashville coffee shop when the editor of the "Modern Love" column emailed that he wanted to print my story.

I felt an entirely new thrill ripple through me as I read and re-read his email.

Holy cow.

I packed up my computer to go home and tell Linda in person.

Three weeks later my writing was in *The Sunday New York Times* and emails poured in from readers all over the world who said they were moved and inspired by the story, and their responses overwhelmingly moved and inspired me. These emails continued to come in for more weeks after the story first appeared.

Linda bought a three-ring notebook and put them all in it for me to keep forever.

The satisfaction I got from having that very personal story read and appreciated by so many people excited me in a way I'd never felt before.

I began to think of my life as a whole, of the other indelible stories and unforgettable people who have made me love most every single day I've been alive. I wanted to weave them all together, for myself and for anyone else who cares.

So, instead of writing songs every day as I had for so many years, I now set out each morning at 7 a.m. for one of my three or four favorite coffee shops in Nashville where I plug in my computer, order coffee, and begin this different kind of writing. Usually seated on all sides are vibrant young people on-the-make in various forms of the music business, the tech and internet world, or some local start-up. Often I can't help overhearing their excited conversations, their hopes and their dreams. Their optimism and energy make me so happy.

Now, many songs and years since the day I dragged my mom's suitcase across the lawn to find my dad in the war, like anyone lucky enough to live a while and have a family, Linda's and my newest stage of life is built on grandchildren, daughters-in-law, and on our three strong and gentle sons who still put their arms around us as we walk down the street.

Traditions remain.

Six days ago, we packed up the car and headed to Watch Hill for our 33rd summer by the sea in the old, weathered house we love so much... the same house we were headed for the night of Linda's accident.

We drove north through the beautiful Shenandoah Valley, then turned right at Harrisburg, PA. Forty minutes later Linda and I came to the place on the interstate where her car had turned over 24 years ago.

The first summer after the accident, when we came to that spot on the highway, I stopped.

I had to.

I got out and walked around. I climbed over the small farm fence to where I'd retrieved some of our CDs a few days after the crash.

They'd been thrown from the car.

After a whole year, incredibly, I found more of our CDs.

There they were, still lying in the field where they'd landed that dark night 12 months before.

With the CDs in my hand, I went back to the grassy area near the road and tried again to reconstruct what might have happened.

That first year, the accident was still so fresh, so new, and for some reason its cause still mattered.

But now, 24 years later, that's not on our minds.

We can't even identify the exact spot anymore.

The small shrubby trees have grown tall.

A guardrail's been built.

The grass is high, and in the last few years we've begun to wonder whether the crash was before or after that nearby mile-marker.

This year, we had nearly reached New York City before we realized we had been listening to an audio book when we passed the scene of the accident.

Late last Thursday afternoon we arrived at our small village of Watch Hill.

As we drove in, we took the long way around.

We slowed down to look at the new hotel.

We drove down past the merry-go-round, past the line at the ice cream window, past our friends' restaurant and then...

Straight ahead stood our house.

"There it is," we both said.

"It looks great," I said, always a little relieved, and a little amazed.

"It does," said Linda.

We pulled our car into its familiar spot next to my small garden and stopped.

"Looks like everything made it through the winter," I said.

Sometimes a high tide creeps up, floods the plants, freezes, and kills all but the most hardy.

"Yes," Linda said, "everything looks very happy."

I carried our light bags inside.

Linda hung up the brightly colored jumpers she'll live in all summer, I put my shorts, socks, etc. in the dresser.

In a few minutes, we'd moved back in.

Downstairs I got out the green wooden mailbox a friend made us the year we bought the house and fastened it to our outside staircase in its long-established spot.

I made a run into the "big city" five miles away for essentials.

Suddenly, we were sitting in our simple white kitchen and a new summer had begun.

Though it was just three days ago now, it could have been 10 years ago.

The scene was timeless:

All six windows are wide open and a breeze is blowing through.

The village green lays out in front of us and just beyond, a snapshot full of sailboats bob and roll at anchor, gilded by evening sunshine.

Fresh-cut flowers sit on our old kitchen table.

Beside me in her wheelchair, Linda has just put out some hummus and pita bread on a platter.

A few friends are coming over.

We have a bunch of Miller Lite and Corona and an endless supply of inexpensive white wine in the refrigerator.

When our friends appear we'll go up on the deck and catch the tail end of the weekly kids' regatta as their tiny sails wend back into the harbor, one behind the other like a string of obedient ducklings.

We'll look out over the water at the fading sun, point out clouds and colors to each other, laugh and talk until it gets dark and the mosquitoes descend.

Yes, there are a few wooden shingles that need replacing and it's about time to sand and re-varnish the frame on the big glass door upstairs.

Paint is chipped on some of these kitchen chairs.

Eventually, I'll get around to that stuff.

But in the meantime, we love this air.

We love this house.

We love this view.

We love this little town.

We love the people who'll be arriving soon.

And we are so grateful to feel all of this.

Because after all we've seen, love is so much better than everything else.

Some mornings now on the porch of this old house, before anyone else is awake, I take a cup of coffee and sit on our top step looking down on the small garden I started 24 years ago. That was the spring following Linda's car accident.

The garden is right at the base of Linda's elevator.

The elevator is in a shaft the builders made to look like the silo of a barn. They covered the shaft with weathered shingles like the rest of our house so it feels like it's always been there.

Not everything I planted in the garden that first year has survived.

But those first lilies are blooming. And two of the sedums are still alive and thriving.

So is the iris.

I just keep planting stuff until something lives.

From this step I can see the window of our bedroom where Linda is sleeping.

Today, like every day, my first thought is how I can help her have a good day, a good life. And I know that her first thought is the same for me.

I'm not an angel. And even though I give it all I've got, I feel I get much more out of living with her than I put into it.

A few minutes ago, I left a thermos of coffee on her night table and a note on her wheelchair. The note says, "I love you so much," with a heart around it and the date at the bottom.

I write a new note each morning.

I write the notes more for me than for her, because I need to tell her how I feel.

And I love to tell her.

The words vary, but the message is always the same.

Sometimes the note is just a string of capital letters that stand for one phrase or another.

By now, she knows most of my letter combinations.

But, she still gets a charge when she solves a new one...like she did with "YAMS" a few days ago.

"You Are My Sunshine!" she called out.

Very pleased with herself.

This morning I sit outside with my laptop.

A few lonely seagulls squawk out over the harbor and in front of me the sun has begun to peek over our rooftop.

I look forward to this day as I have to so many others, and I think of all the surprises and acts of love, and kindness, and strokes of pure luck that have put us in this wonderful place on earth.

Sometimes, if my mind wanders, and nobody stops by, and the newspaper guy is late, my thoughts pull up fresh pictures from the past.

My mom died last year. She lived to be 95…a very savvy person to the end.

A few years ago she said, "How do you think you and Linda kept it together after her accident?"

I smiled.

"Mom," I said, "do you remember when I was about 15, feeling my oats, thinking I'd seen it all and could cope with anything because I was already so worldly and experienced?"

She laughed. "No, not really," she said.

"Yes," I said. "You said, 'Honey, be careful, because whatever got you the last time will not be what gets you the next time'."

Her eyes got wide.

"What?" she said.

"Yes! And you were right. I paid attention because you were the one who let me loose in the first place."

"You're giving me credit where…"

"Mom," I said, "if you hadn't let me go make mistakes, have adventures, 10 million things that have happened since would've been debilitating shocks, but you let me out in the world early and I learned how to survive, overcome things. Linda and I wanted each other so badly that we'd do anything we had to do to be together. But the reason I could hold up my end was because from day one you let me learn how to do that."

Now she smiled.

"Layng," she said, "sometimes I think you're delusional."

I smiled back.

"If so, it's your fault."

She blushed.

"That's not what I expected to hear," she said, "but thank you."

Nobody spoke.

"And it did help that we paid no attention to statistics or dire predictions," I said.

"Statistics from who?"

"From whoever studies that stuff. The doctor told us the odds were 80% that we'd get divorced in the first two years."

Linda sat next to me the day we heard that.

In the room were seven other people in wheelchairs.

Being a paraplegic was new to all of them.

This was a class in what to expect from now on, in our new lives.

How to cope.

How to survive.

Spouses were encouraged to attend.

The doctor speaking to us was our favorite.

"That's the statistic," he repeated, "80% of you. Two years."

Linda and I had no illusions about the unknowns, the daily trials, the heartaches that lay ahead.

But we never even talked about that statistic.

"I remember hearing it and feeling it had nothing to do with us," I said to my mom.

The doctor was kind.

He cared deeply.

He knew most of those in the wheelchairs no longer had feeling from the waist or chest down.

"I'm sorry to say that sex, as you know it, is over," he said.

The woman in front of us was reading *The Enquirer*, chewing gum, her purse slung over the back of her folding chair.

She flipped the page. Didn't appear to have heard.

Her husband sat next to her in his wheelchair.

A ladybug crawled across his knee. He smacked it.

"Sometimes," the doctor continued, "a woman will feel sexually aroused by being touched just below the breast. But everyone is different, so...not always."

Notes were not needed for revelations like this.

We never missed those classes. They were every Thursday at 2 p.m.

There was so much to know. Soon enough, we'd be out of the hospital to handle this new life alone.

Across the room, a newly minted cripple sat on his power wheelchair. A day-glo orange flag on a whip aerial poked up behind his seat. The flag jerked slightly as the man impatiently punched the powerchair's "Forward" button.

He had no spouse.

He was staring out the window.

"Next week we'll discuss household dangers," said the doctor, "irons, coffee, heaters. Things that will burn right through you without you even feeling them. Please try to be here."

Such lessons and exercises of all kinds consumed us.

Linda learned how to go downstairs backwards in her wheelchair in case of fire.

The day she came back from that class I said, "Can you really do that?"

"Yes," she said.

She could do that, and anything else necessary, no matter how impossible it looked. She learned how to pop her wheelchair over a door jam or up a curb. She learned how to slide on a board from her wheelchair onto a bed or a car seat. She learned how to fold up her wheelchair, pull it into the car behind her seat, drive wherever she wants to go, get the chair out, get in it and go get her hair cut or whatever.

I was never much for blood or peeks inside the body.

But I got over it.

I learned a lot about female plumbing, largely to understand why and how catheterization works.

Since all feeling below Linda's bustline was gone, there would be no "tingle" to let her know it's time to urinate. So, to prevent surprises, she would now catheterize herself every three hours.

I learned how to do that for her, if needed.

Since her bowels no longer functioned, she would now have to reach up inside herself and "bring down" by hand what formerly came down by itself.

Linda learned how to do that.

With practice, I learned how to do that for her, too.

Now Linda does that for herself every third day.

Of all the skills she's mastered, the most basic is also one of the most impressive.

Dressing herself.

Initially, getting dressed took about 45 minutes.

Huh?

Imagine. Your body moves only from the chest up. You have to lift yourself and get your skirt under you…never mind pulling it out and getting it even and centered. Then, imagine doing that when you've just come out of the shower and your body is damp, your clothes sticking to you.

Seeing Linda do this, now in about four minutes, is still one of the most moving sights I've ever seen.

That and her smile.

I feel it's always there.

By the time she "comes downstairs" in the morning it seems she's already done more hard things than I'll do before dark.

Yet she'll never mention those things.

They're not what she's thinking about.

She's much more likely to do what she did yesterday.

She rolled down the hall with her twinkling eyes, popped across the threshold, gave me the once-over, and said, "Well…who's this cute guy in my kitchen?"

And, once again, I did what I'll do until the day I die.

Melt.

EPILOGUE

At sunset these days, we sit on the deck of our house in Watch Hill in our side-by-side chairs — mine Adirondack-style, Linda's on wheels — and we look across the water at Fishers Island and think we are as lucky as two people can be.

We don't know what will happen tomorrow, or who will live how long. But we were young together. We struggled to make a life. We raised three great sons. We've each been the caregiver and the cared-for, and I suspect that we each have a little more of both in our future.

We are two, but we are one. And I love those numbers.

ACKNOWLEDGEMENTS

———————

This book was vastly improved by comments, suggestions, and encouragement from many friends and relatives. My wife Linda always made time to read new writing, lived through at least 100 versions of every sentence, and not once had trouble being both frank and encouraging. The magnificent Beth Stein edited the book with the clearest of thinking, subtlety, warmth, and with boundless faith in the book's story. Beth also came up with the book's title "PERMISSION TO FLY" which rang true the second she said it. Along the way, priceless feedback was given to me by Layng Martine III, Tucker Martine, Mac Martine, Gene Martine, Suzanne Martine, John Martine, Anne Martine, Jean Martine, Layng Martine Sr., Lee and Sharon Schilling, Shannon Sneed, Laura Veirs, Chris Hassel, H. Jackson Brown Jr., Robert Hicks, Bobby Braddock, Laura Knox, Gary Fisketjon, Dan Jones, Bill and Robin King, Charlie and Janis Feldman, Penny Kelly, Rodes and Lindy Fishburne, Peter Guralnick, John Pritchard, Hilary Heminway, John Heminway, Mary Margaret Johnson, Kathy Nolan Holaday, Barry Nolan, Robin and Chris Donohoe, Sharon Collinson, Tina Barney, Lonnie and Olga Goff, Bobby Eastman, Allison and John Beasley, Chuck and Deborah Royce, Clara Bass, Nancy and Wayland Holyfield, John Stein, Julie Schoerke, Bob McDill, Jennifer Kimball, Charlie Atwood, Judy Smith, Jan and Chip Raymond, Diane and Tom Smith, Nina and Billy Weil, Ken Paulson, Rick and Heidi Worcester, Margaret Renkl, Cindy Uh, Richard

Greene, Kirk Reynolds, Gayle Restivo, Bill Tomson, Kristin Russell, Sam Calagione, Clare Pelino, Tania Clark, Bobbie Allardyce, Michael Kosser, Mary and Rick Johnson, Jane Dystel, Jan Simenson, Susan Stewart, Karen and Keith LaRose, Jacques de Spoelberch, Tom and Margah Lips, Karen and David Conrad, Rita and Rory Bourke, Richard and Sherry Mainegra, Lindsay Bohannon, Michelle Tessler, John Van Mol, Cee and Paul Verbinnen, Glen Edelstein, Max Goldberg, Joan Lemp, Donna and Grant Simmons, John and Fatima Penrose, Tom Draper, Bill Batty, Rachel Draper, Ilona Holland, Dookie Crater Tingue, David Battis, John Baeder, Sheila O'Donnell, Ed Russell, Katie Brown, Yvonne Lieblein, Rob and Carol Stein, Richard Leigh, Even Stevens, John Lowenberg, Jeff Chapple, Carrie Pelzel, Bruce McClintock, Kathy Robbins, John and Anne Clay, Lauren Braddock, Louise and Sonny Curtis, Kate and John Townsend, Nancy and Terry Ellsberry, David Kirk, Jeff Matthews, Sharon Bush, Bob Murray, Christie and Francis Jenkins, Karin McCormick, Sarah Goff, Justin Goff, Edith Eglin, Richard and Beth Courtney, Carolyn and Del Bryant, Jeanne and John Blasberg, Pat Richins, Judy and Walter Lentz, Pat Alger, Susan and Mike Reid, Jack and Marcia Felber, Don and Kristin Taylor, MJ and Victor Orsinger, Earline and Dale Morris, Troy Tomlinson, Jody Williams, Bart Herbison, Jill and Chris Wight, Ray Stevens, Buddy Kalb, David Wilds, Cal Turner, Lewis Anderson, Susan St. Romain, Jeanne and Gino Marchetti, Jenny Breeden, Ann Lyle, Sherry Howell, Scott Gunter, Charlie Black, Bobby Fischer, Ginny Johnson, Will Robinson, Scott Swift, Jennifer and Andrew Nathan, Samantha Saturn, Samantha Spector, Steve Mason, Dusty Ryan, Ray Mott, Bob and Rob Richins, Shelley Harwell, Craig Wiseman, Kathy Green, Sister Kate Lamb, Marcia Mallard, George and Kren Teren, Cole Wilson, George and Penny Hart, Brenna Mader, Steve O'Brien, Jessi Baker, David and Lynn Leach, John Campbell, Craig Gossage, Ned Schwentker, Nancy Cobb, Jack and Marguerite Lynch, Bill and Michele Matzinger.

My brilliant and endlessly patient brother, Gene, designed the book's cover, our logo, prepared all photographs for printing and has been my true sounding board for family memories. I cannot imagine attempting this book without him.

NOTES

RUB IT IN, c. 1971 Ahab Music, by Layng Martine Jr.
LIFE IS A WILD PLACE, c. 2005 Layng Martine Jr. Songs, by Layng
Martine Jr.

CPSIA information can be obtained
at www.ICGtesting.com
Printed in the USA
LVHW111508101019
633801LV00006B/60/P